C000099396

At David C Cook, we equip the local church around
the corner and around the globe to make disciples.
Come see how we are working together—go to
www.davidccook.org. Thank you!

transforming lives together

What people are saying about …

SCATTERED SERVANTS

"When Alan Scott speaks, I try to listen. Where he leads, I try to follow. And now that he's writing, I'm reading and cheering him on. *Scattered Servants* is that rarest of things: a book that is necessary. If I had my way, every church leader in the country would be required to read it at least twice."

Pete Greig, founder of 24-7 Prayer
International, Emmaus Rd, Guildford

"Few voices I know are engaging the issue of city transformation and the church's role with the conviction and clarity that Alan Scott does in *Scattered Servants*. Revival was never meant to only be a set of meetings confined to a church building. Revival has always been a move of God's Spirit that awakens the church with a passion for those who are away from Jesus and a passion to see the community they live and work in transformed. This book comes from years of seeing God move in profound ways through a church that was committed to revival through serving their city. As a leader and a pastor, I have both been challenged and inspired by Alan's leadership and call to see the church empowered and equipped to reach their cities. I am grateful he has written this book and believe deeply this is a message the body of Christ must hear and embrace if we are to see revival in our day."

Banning Liebscher, Jesus
Culture founder and pastor

"*Scattered Servants* is a magnificent and truly prophetic book. If we are to reach our world with the good news of Jesus, the church has to stop throwing Bible grenades from a safe distance and get involved. Out of the building and into the streets. Alan writes biblically, passionately, and practically. He lives what he writes. It is scriptural and it works. It is time to regain our confidence in the power of the gospel to save men and women and also to transform society."

Rev. Canon Mike Pilavachi, cofounder
and leader of Soul Survivor

"Alan Scott is a wonderful, gifted communicator. Having been friends for many years, I'm excited about *Scattered Servants* being released. It will inspire and impact you. Prepare to receive as you open these pages."

Robby Dawkins, author, international
conference speaker, and film subject

"As I read this book, I could feel faith and hope pumping through my veins! Here is a Kingdom vision that has the power to release the church to truly bless and transform cities. This book will inspire, unsettle, and I believe profoundly impact the way you follow Christ. It certainly did that for me!"

Tim Hughes, worship leader,
singer, and songwriter

"We are at a pivotal moment in the life of the American church. Scandal, decline, and compromise seem to dominate the headlines. Into the heart of this moment Alan has written a prophetic and powerful book to call the church back to its redemptive potential and promise. This book is brimming with hope, moving stories, theological insight, and practical tools to equip the people of God for mission. I believe this will be a real gift to the body of Christ in this urgent hour."

Jon Tyson, lead pastor of Church of the City
New York and author of *The Burden Is Light*

"Very few leaders think like Alan Scott. Even less *live* like Alan Scott. His wide, expansive vision of transformation, not just for churches, but for entire cities, hits a deep nerve in my soul. A very hungry part of me says *yes*. And his humble, yet powerful person is even more compelling. Seeing Alan's community in Northern Ireland cast a vision in my mind of what could be here in America. But being with Alan is what's sparked a desire to open up every moment of every day to the Spirit's work in my own city. This is a voice we need to hear."

John Mark Comer, pastor of teaching
and vision at Bridgetown Church

ALAN
SCOTT

SCATTERED SERVANTS

UNLEASHING THE CHURCH
TO BRING LIFE TO THE CITY

DAVID C COOK

transforming lives together

SCATTERED SERVANTS
Published by David C Cook
4050 Lee Vance Drive
Colorado Springs, CO 80918 U.S.A.

Integrity Music Limited, a Division of David C Cook
Eastbourne, East Sussex BN23 6NT, England

The graphic circle C logo is a registered trademark of David C Cook.

Unless otherwise noted, Scripture quotations are taken from THE HOLY
BIBLE, NEW INTERNATIONAL VERSION®, NIV® Copyright © 1973, 2011
by Biblica, Inc.® Used by permission. All rights reserved worldwide. Scripture
quotations marked TLB are taken from The Living Bible, copyright © 1971. Used
by permission of Tyndale House Publishers, Inc., Carol Stream, Illinois 60188. All
rights reserved; THE MESSAGE are taken from THE MESSAGE. Copyright © by
Eugene H. Peterson 1993, 2002. Used by permission of Tyndale House Publishers,
Inc.; NIVUK are taken from Holy Bible, New International Version® Anglicized,
NIV® Copyright © 1979, 2011 by Biblica, Inc.® Used by permission. All rights
reserved worldwide; and NLT are taken from the *Holy Bible*, New Living Translation,
copyright © 1996, 2015 by Tyndale House Foundation. Used by permission of
Tyndale House Publishers, Inc., Carol Stream, Illinois 60188. All rights reserved.

Details in some stories have been changed to protect
the identities of the persons involved.

LCCN 2018942852
ISBN 978-0-8307-7585-9
eISBN 978-0-8307-7586-6

© 2018 Alan Scott

The Team: Ian Matthews, Keith Wall, Nick Lee, Susan Murdock
Cover Design: Mark Prentice, beatroot.media
Cover Photo: iStock

Printed in the United Kingdom
First Edition 2018

2 3 4 5 6 7 8 9 10

090618

This book is dedicated to the Scattered Servants of Causeway Coast Vineyard, whose faith inspires me and whose hope is inscribed in the lives and landscape of our community. Your love for the Father is beautiful. Thank you for trusting us with your hearts. Thank you for letting us be part of your journey. Thank you for reminding me that greatness is not the domain of the strong but of the servant. Thank you for giving us a place to belong and to dream beyond ourselves. I hope this story, your story, invites us all into more.

CONTENTS

LOVING THE CITY BACK TO LIFE

I didn't grow up in church. I grew up in the city. I grew up desperately hurting and secretly hoping that another life was available. It wasn't until I became a believer at age fifteen that the church became the refuge from the city my soul longed for. It loved me back to life.

Since that time, I've spent my life serving Jesus in and through the local church. The thing that has surprised me, though, is the further I've stepped into the story of God, the more Jesus has wrecked my heart for the city. Indeed, there is a longing in the heart of God that His church would not only be a refuge *from* the city, but also a refuge *for* the city itself.

Scattered Servants is a book about bringing life to the city.

It is written from a context of outpouring, describing the journey of the local church in Northern Ireland I had the privilege of pastoring for almost twenty years, where miracles were happening regularly and hundreds were coming to faith on the streets. It is a book about the church loving the city back to life ... about unleashing the church to bring life to the city. It reminds us that our cities are not hard to reach—they are just hard to reach when we stay in the building.

Indeed, it's impossible to reach our cities through better church services. While gathered environments (such as Sunday services and small groups) can grow the church, only scattered servants can bring life to broken cities. It is time to unlock kingdom identity, kingdom authority, and kingdom ministry. It is time to unleash the power of everyone, everywhere, everyday so that the church begins to fill every city, every industry, and every family with the beauty and story of Christ. If that's your hunger, I invite you to take the next step into the story:

> Join God on the journey of bringing life to your city.
> Demonstrate the power of God beyond the building.
> Discover the dreams God has put in your heart for the sake of your city.
> Move on in your faith and move out in God's favor.
> Understand your identity and unlock your authority.
> Develop a faith that isn't just strong enough to survive culture but that is bold enough to transform it.

The dream of God over your life is not that you become a believer and help out the local church. The dream of God over your life is that you come alive in His presence and bring life to every environment, spilling contagious hope into hurting humanity.

And as you read this book, my prayer is that you would be awakened to dream in partnership with God over your own city—in ways you've not dreamed before, in ways that renew culture and birth hope in the heart of the city beyond the walls of the church. Because the next great move of God is not a movement *in* the church but a movement *of* the church.

Chapter 1

THE SPIRIT RESTS
UPON THE SERVANTS

As Danny shared his frustration, I knew it would be a recurring conversation. He loved his church, he loved the relevancy of the teaching, and he loved the accessible environment. But he missed a sense of potency in his own life. Sunday morning gatherings helped him understand his life, but they didn't empower him to bring life to others. Danny wanted more. He wanted to see God's kingdom advance through his heart and hands. He wanted to lead people to faith in the office, not just invite them to church.

A similar conversation happened with Kim, and I knew it too would be a recurring theme. She loved her church. She loved the freedom, the sense of intimacy during worship, and the vision of empowered community. Sunday morning gatherings provided great environments for expression and equipping. But she couldn't imagine bringing her friends and family. She desperately wanted to see salvation—people coming to Jesus. Lots of them.

Danny and Kim both wondered, *What if?*

What if believers didn't have to choose between churches that emphasized "seeker sensitive" or "supernaturally empowered"?

What if gathered environments were marked by God's presence and scattered servants were empowered by His Spirit?

What if it was normal for people to come to faith in the building?

What if it was normal for miracles to happen beyond the building?

What if our services attracted the lost and empowered the found?

Whenever those "what-if" questions surface in conversation with leaders, I usually begin my response with the same sentence (paraphrasing pastor Erwin McManus): "It's not difficult to reach the community. It's just really hard to change the church." Our cities are longing for life. But to reach them, we have to reposition our churches.

It's not hard to have people come to faith in our services. But the call is to *go*.

It's not especially hard to grow a church. Yet church growth should not be the highest goal.

It's not hard to make disciples. But the call is to make disciples who change cities.

It's not difficult to raise up impressive structures. But the call is to raise sons and daughters who will serve the King of Kings.

It's not especially challenging to create irresistible gathered environments. But the call is to release unstoppable, impassioned scattered servants.

Let me introduce you to a scattered servant named Ben. He was visiting a family in our church when he noticed a group of young men drinking beer. He sensed the Holy Spirit prompt him to talk to them. Locking eyes with the guy who appeared to be the leader of this bunch, Ben declared, "You are drinking because you split from your girlfriend two days ago. Is that correct?"

The man's eyes widened suddenly, and he nodded in assent.

"Jesus sent me with a message for you," Ben said. "He told me that you are just like me. You gave up rugby a few months ago due to an ACL injury, and you have been grieving because you can't play anymore." Then Ben lifted his trouser leg to reveal the surgical scar from his own ACL damage.

By now the young man and his friends were in shock.

"You are also like me," Ben continued, "because your dad is a minister and my dad is a minister. Is that right?"

The man nodded, his mouth hanging open.

"I would like to pray with you," Ben said. And he did.

I'll tell you about another scattered servant named Nick. He was out shopping with his wife when he sensed God prompt him to approach two young women. Unsure how to start a conversation, Nick waited for God to reveal Himself. Then he said to one of the women, "I think you have a tattoo on your arm." The lady laughed. After all, it's not uncommon for people to have tattoos on their arms, and Nick's pronouncement hardly represented spectacular insight.

Undaunted, Nick continued: "Your tattoo is a name. It's the name of your daughter. You lost her." Unable to retain her composure any longer, the woman began weeping and soon poured out her story of loss. After talking with Nick for a long while, she opened her life to Christ.

Now, imagine a church with everyone leading the community into life through the empowering of the Holy Spirit. A church with everyone reaching the "unreachable." A church with everyone risking to do the "impossible." A church with everyone giving everything to help people say yes to God.

Although I have the privilege of leading this kind of church, it hasn't always been that way. It took a long time to learn that God is doing more beyond the church than He is in church.

God's Work beyond Church Walls

In the spring of 2006, a tourist from the South of Ireland came to our church in Coleraine, on the northern coast. The woman told our prayer team that, while giving birth, she had been given an epidural injection for pain relief. Usually a safe procedure, in this case it had left the young mother paralyzed below the waist.

Moved with compassion, the team prayed earnestly and confidently. Still, there seemed to be no substantial change. They told her that healing can occur in three ways: sometimes people are healed instantaneously, other times they are healed gradually over a long period of time, and occasionally they are healed soon after they leave a service or prayer meeting.

A few days later, as this woman traveled back to her home in Southern Ireland, she felt a sensation in her legs. She urgently told her husband, who was driving their car, "Pull over! Something's happening!" A few moments later, the woman got out of the car and started walking. And then running. Her paralysis had been healed.

She was free to run toward a different future than she had imagined could be possible.

News of this woman's miraculous transformation reached us when friends of hers came to Coleraine to be prayed for by the team. It seemed her story was creating a stir in her town. Later that spring as I reflected on her story, I began to feel strangely uncomfortable.

What if her story was God's way of enlarging our church's vision and heart for the South of Ireland? What if God was waiting to do more in her town? What if we took a team to her town and simply showed up? What if there was a movement hidden inside a moment? What if God's initial invitation to go after the lost extended beyond our borders and our area? And yet what if we went there and nothing happened? Or worse yet, what if the Catholic community perceived us as being typical Protestants trying to convert them?

There were so many questions swirling in our minds. But we sensed the Lord's leading. We had to go. So on one unforgettable day—June 17, 2006—we set out.

Within ten minutes of erecting a banner that read "HEALING," we were praying for people. About an hour later, a woman who suffered with diabetes causing partial blindness asked if we would pray for her. We had never seen anyone healed of blindness, but as we prayed and her family watched, her sight was restored.

Suddenly, it seemed that everyone wanted prayer. The woman just healed brought her eight-year-old son, whose leg was misshapen. As a result, the boy walked with a pronounced limp. One member of our team prayed, and immediately the leg was healed. Moments later, the boy's uncle arrived complaining of a burning sensation in his lungs that made breathing difficult. He was clearly in pain. We invited him to take a seat while the team prayed. Someone commanded the pain to go and the lungs to open. He experienced instant healing.

We found ourselves in the center of the city and in the middle of a move of God.

After many more healings, the woman whose sight was restored asked if we would go to her mother's home. A few of our team members went. They described the scene as similar to the story of the healing of the paralytic in the New Testament (Luke 5). The people there had contacted their extended family, with so many arriving that there was barely any room in the house. Our team prayed for one little boy bent over due to severe scoliosis. As they prayed, his spine straightened. Faith in God's power permeated the room, and many other people were healed of various conditions and ailments.

As wonderful as the healings were, what gripped my heart most were the words of the mother. She was a Catholic woman, the matriarch of her family. She told us that at seven o'clock that morning (the exact time we left our town to journey toward hers), she knelt at her bedside and asked God to send someone to help her family that day. God heard her cry, and in His great mercy healed her two grandsons, her son, her two daughters, and several other family members.

We were privileged to participate in God's restorative power that day. The long journey home gave me time to reflect, and one thought dominated my mind: What would have happened to that family had we not shown up? What if we had stayed home in our comfortable, familiar environments? I already knew the answer.

From Gathered Environments to Scattered Servants

It's hard to reach a city when we stay in the building and when our ministry models revolve around expanding our services. Gathered environments grow churches; scattered servants reach cities. When I use the term *scattered servants*, I mean a movement of people empowered by the Holy Spirit and sent to bring life to cities. When they show up in the city, carrying hope for the city, everything changes and captives are released.

I recall a woman named Jennifer, who had suffered from fibromyalgia for many years. The condition caused depression for her and anguish for her husband. Unable to leave her home for months at a time, she was losing touch with reality. But all of that was about to change. One Friday night, Jennifer had a dream in which she was standing in the center of our town. As she looked up, she saw a lady with short hair wearing a brown coat. Behind the lady was a huge banner that simply said, "HEALING." The next morning, Jennifer decided to head into town, where our team had already gathered and begun to pray for the sick. As she stood at the center of our town, she saw our banner and a lady with short, dark hair.

Thinking it to be more than coincidence, Jennifer tentatively approached the team. After she poured out her story, the team members offered to pray. Years of pain were washed away in a moment of grace, as the pain caused by fibromyalgia left her body. The next day, Jennifer and her husband sat in church as we continued our sermon series on "Living beyond the Shadow of Depression." This couple was ambushed by a God who is both Lord of the church and Lord of the harvest.

What's New Is Old

Today there is a shift from gathered environments to scattered servants. But it's not a new thing. As we read in the book of Acts,

> Those who had been scattered preached the word wherever they went. Philip went down to a city in Samaria and proclaimed the Messiah there. When the crowds heard Philip and saw the signs he performed, they all paid close attention to what he said. For with shrieks, impure spirits came out of many, and many who were paralyzed or lame were healed. So there was great joy in that city. (8:4–8)

Those who had been scattered preached (communicated and demonstrated) the word (the message of the kingdom) wherever they went. Those who had been scattered introduced the gospel. Those who had been scattered began bringing life to the city, finding ways to leave the kingdom in every heart. What was improbable in gathered environments became possible through scattered servants. The mission no longer centered on strategic locations; the mission happened in everyday, ordinary moments.

The movement was unleashed.

The movement was unstoppable.

The movement was unpredictable.

Servants brought life everywhere they went. Every environment became subject to the influence of hope carried in the hearts and hands of these early believers. *Gathering* together as believers had given them access to exceptional teaching and astonishing generosity, but *going* together had given them authority to bring hope to hurting humanity.

Fast-forward a few centuries. In the nation of Ireland, another band of scattered servants emerged—early Celtic missionaries—convinced that God was doing more beyond their shore, beyond their lives. A few miles west of where I lived for many years, those devoted servants would set out in rugged little boats known as corracles. They had no programs or models to offer. They hoisted sails and invited the wind to blow them ... wherever.

And wherever they went, those who had been scattered preached (communicated and demonstrated) the word (the message of the kingdom). Astonishing! Before long, signs and wonders followed—and new communities flourished.

Amazingly, those missionaries conducted no demographic studies and no market research to identify the most responsive communities. I can imagine a reporter of the day asking, "Where are you going?" And the response would be, "It doesn't matter. Wherever we go, the kingdom will come. When we get there, we know that God's Spirit will be present and powerful." And it happened just as they believed. Whole cities encountered the King and His kingdom.

It's tempting to consign these stories to the pages of history. Yet they are designed to reveal what is possible in our day—biblical, historical, and cultural reminders that the kingdom comes as we go. We stand in a long line of believers who brought life to whole communities. Not only is it possible and normal, it is also our purpose and nature.

In our town, in our day, we are daring to dream of atmospheric shifts over our city. We are once again discovering the potency of the kingdom to bring life to the city. We are moving beyond gathered environments and entrusting the kingdom to scattered servants who communicate and demonstrate the word—the message of the kingdom—wherever they go.

The next move of God is not a movement *in* the church. It is a movement *of* the church.

Programs Don't Change a City—People Do

Brian lost his job during the recession, but he didn't lose his job because of the recession; he lost his job because of his compassion. He was helping people find Jesus in his workplace. His employers couldn't condone his actions, so they fired him. Eventually he got another job in Belfast, in a community considered difficult to reach and impervious to change. Nobody told Brian, though, and because he wasn't from the area, he did what he always does. He began bringing life. After leading some of the residents to faith, he started to dream of ways to reach more people. He decided to hold an event in his workplace for the broken seeking belonging.

This time his employer gave him permission to explore the idea. So Brian asked God to give him favor with the paramilitaries who controlled the community and to open the hearts of people who lived in the area.

After praying, he went from house to house inviting folks. As he did, one lady opened her door and her heart. Her son had recently taken his own life, and she was overwhelmed by the loss. She didn't want anyone to experience the same grief. Therefore, she promised to do everything she could so that her neighborhood could hear good news.

And she did.

More than seventy local people showed up. Six of them committed to follow Jesus.

As a church leadership team, we wouldn't have and couldn't have designed that moment. It didn't seem safe or sensible. It wasn't part of our strategic plan, but God put it in the heart of a scattered servant.

Broken Cities Need Something More Than Bigger Churches

The great late-1800s preacher E. M. Bounds was right when he said, "Men and women have always been God's method."[1] And sometimes the kids get in on the action too.

A friend named Amanda went shopping at Ikea one day and dragged her kids along. As they all neared the checkout, Amanda was preoccupied and didn't notice that each of her three girls had already lost interest in the experience and had gone looking for adventure. After Amanda paid for her goods, she looked up and witnessed her kids do something more bold than she would ever do—something she probably wouldn't have given permission to do. Her girls were praying for a blind woman. Nobody had instructed them to pray. It wasn't a church gathering. It wasn't a mission trip. It wasn't even family devotions. It was children commissioned by their Father in heaven to bring release to the broken.

I recall the story of Rory, who took his seat for a test beside his best friend, George. As they settled in, Rory leaned over and said, "I would like to pray with you." George, perhaps more focused on the test (as Rory should have been), misheard him and replied, "Yes, yes, we will play later at break time." Undeterred, Rory repeated his offer to pray. "No, I would like to pray for you right now."

This time George heard him and agreed, presumably thinking that Rory would pray for him and the test he was facing. Instead, Rory did what scattered servants do. Leaning closer to his friend, he whispered, "Father, I take authority over epilepsy. I forbid it, and I command it to go in Your name." He then got on with his test.

Last I heard, George hasn't had an epileptic seizure since that moment.

I'm not sure how either lad did in the test.

Life comes through scattered servants, whether young or old or any age in between. Our gatherings of believers grow the church; scattered servants change the community.

Broken cities need more than bigger churches.

Broken cities need more than better services.

Broken cities need a new reality, an alternative story.

Broken cities don't just need culturally relevant churches.

Broken cities need the church to show up beyond the building.

Broken cities need tender hearts who show up with love and grace.

We can't impress our cities into life, but we can immerse them in the life to come. We can bring back life. However, developing life-giving churches at the center of the city involves more than creating irresistible environments marked by excellence and service. Any human industry can accomplish those goals. Life-giving churches are defined by the life of another world—the life and joy they bring to the city.[2] God has promised joy to the world. He is waiting for kingdom servants to drag the promise to the surface. When they show up, there is great joy in the city.

Catching Up with a Move of God

Let's return to the story I started earlier about the gypsy family in the South of Ireland. A few days after praying for this family, we found ourselves once again traveling the five hours to pray for other members of the traveling community. We spent three hours among people who were incredibly friendly and exceptionally hungry for God. To my knowledge, none of them were pursuers of Him. As we were about to pray for one woman, she stretched out her hand and asked me to bless two pieces of material. I now know these are called "Padre Pio," but at the time I had no idea. I knew they had spiritual significance for her, and I knew they were part of the Catholic tradition.

At that point I had lived in Northern Ireland for eight years, and I knew that I was not supposed to pray over icons. Prayer = good. Icons = bad. Everything in my Christian background and heritage led me away from what God seemed to be directing me to do in that moment. It was as if I said to Him, "God, I can't do what You are asking me to do, because You wouldn't want me to do it." But I had the choice to either reach out to those God was reaching for or to hide behind my tradition. A flood of thoughts rushed through my mind, yet out of my mouth came the words, "I would love to pray."

As I started to pray, I felt prompted by the Holy Spirit, who seemed to be saying to me, "She has two sons, and they don't get along with each another. It's breaking her heart. Tell her that I know." So I stopped praying and told the lady, "Just as you wear these two icons close to your heart, so you have two sons, and their fighting is breaking your heart." As I relayed to her what I felt God was saying, she began to weep. And as she wept, I felt God speak to me a second time, this time more personally. As He spoke, something inside me snapped. He said, "Son, you were so busy correcting her theology, and all I wanted to do was connect with her heart. Learn My ways."

His ways were different from the approach I would have used. I would have explained the inadequacies of her theology and the sufficiency of Christ alone, but I wasn't in the driver's seat—He was. It is entirely His prerogative how He chooses to lead people to Himself. The task of scattered servants is not to question *how* God moves but to move with Him *as* He moves. The way we *think* God should move must not interfere with the way He is actually moving. Our role is to pursue Him in what He is already doing, not convince Him of the merits of what we have been doing.

Right now as you read this book, God is looking for ways to help people connect with His purpose for their lives. God is inviting people all over your community to take a spiritual journey from their pain and brokenness, abuse and abandonment, isolation and fear, and bring them into a close connection with Him. Our role is simply to partner with Him, to work together to release what is good. Our role is not to win the lost. Our role is to leave the building in pursuit of the One who lives among the low and the contrite, the humble and the despised, the needy and the thirsty.

Our role is to move when He moves.

It's what scattered servants do.

Chapter 2

AMONG THE PEOPLE

"God, I can't settle for this. This isn't going to be enough for me."

It was a curious prayer, but it had gripped my heart for months. On the outside, everything was going well. People were gathering, our congregation was growing, and (until eight weeks previously) I'd thought we were leading a thriving church.

But inside something was breaking.

I stood in my room weeping, unsure of what lay ahead but clear I couldn't stay where I was. I picked up my Bible, turning again to a passage that had become all too familiar.

"If all this had been too little, I would have given you even more."[1]

In that moment I sensed Him say, "Son, I am not offended when you ask for more, only when you settle for less."

My frustration and His invitation were colliding. Things were changing.

Weekdays, I kept praying. Sundays, I kept preaching. I hid my growing dissatisfaction from the congregation, not yet ready to expose them to the fire consuming my private thoughts. No one else noticed. We were good at "doing church." Kathryn could lead worship. I could teach a little. Ministry times were powerful. And for a while I was satisfied as long as those realities remained the same.

Then divine disruption entered my world.

God began speaking about His friends far from church. I realized my concerns and His weren't the same, though I naively thought they were. This was what was breaking my heart. I had grieved His heart by ignoring His heart. I had ignored His heart by forgetting those who were far from Him. The evidence was undeniable. Our church had gathered together for four years without one person coming to faith. I'm ashamed to say it didn't bother me—until God spoke.

When He spoke, I broke. Again I prayed: "God, ministry isn't going to be enough for me. A growing church isn't going to do it for me. I don't want more of the same. And I don't want to lead a church that doesn't lean toward the lost. Put in me Your passion for the lost."

The following January, in 2003, we gathered our leaders. Each year we did the same thing—retreated with our core leaders to surrender once more to the divine invitation over our lives. But this time was different. This time would change everything.

I remember it vividly. We huddled together in a dilapidated building, dreaming of shaping an alternative future. As we prayed our best prayers, God spoke through His people. One by one our leaders shared their sense of God's voice among us. And then, one of our more soft-spoken leaders summoned her courage and raised her voice.

"I think I had a vision," she said. "I saw a large group of kids dressed in black, unaware of God's plan for their life. They march to a drumbeat of death, destruction, desolation, and depression. Every time these words are spoken, another kid along the line becomes dressed in black. In their path are hurdles at various intervals. As the kids approach the obstacles, some make it over while others struggle to make it. When they can't, they slit their wrists and fall down. Meanwhile the others keep walking. Another hurdle, more fall, the others keep walking. There is no reason for life. No hope. The music drives them to cut themselves, while great confusion and fear reign in their hearts."

The rest of us listened, captivated, as she continued. "Surrounding them are fields and a forest, and in the forest is another group, all dressed in white. Like the others, their music moves them as they dance along slowly, singing quietly. They are at peace, yet they are looking for something, always looking. As they come to the edge of a hillside, they look down into the valley and see the dark line of kids. They cry out to one another, 'We've found them, we've found them!' And they run toward them.

"As I look, I brace myself for the battle ahead. Yet as the two sides meet, there is no battle. Instead, the white army surrounds those in darkness and walk among them. They speak of a new destiny, singing over them, praying with them, touching their hands, and blessing them. They lift those who have fallen and bind their wrists with bandages. As they do so, in this atmosphere of joy, what is 'on them' comes on the others, and those once defined by despair begin singing and dancing. And then I notice they, too, have become dressed in white. That's it. That's what I saw."

We all sat there, stunned.

It was more than a moment. It was a mandate.

As our retreat ended, everyone knew we couldn't continue to do things the way we had been. God was doing something different with us. We could never allow our love for lost people to slide again. Together we sensed a fresh commission: "If you will go after those on the outside, I will look after those on the inside." In effect, God was saying, "The future of this church depends upon bringing life to lost people."

It was time to move among the people.

Answering the Call to Be "Among"

Frequently in the New Testament, we encounter the phrase "among the people." It is how Jesus started His ministry:

> Jesus went throughout Galilee, teaching in their synagogues, proclaiming the good news of the kingdom, and healing every disease and sickness among the people. News about him spread all over Syria, and people brought to him all who were ill, with various diseases, those suffering severe pain, the demon-possessed, those having seizures, and the paralyzed; and he healed them.[2]

> When the people saw the mutes speaking, the maimed healthy, the paraplegics walking around, the blind looking around, they were astonished

and let everyone know that God was blazingly alive among them.[3]

And this conviction was the environment where apostolic power was most evident, as the early church took to the streets:

> The apostles performed many signs and wonders among the people. And all the believers used to meet together in Solomon's Colonnade. No one else dared join them, even though they were highly regarded by the people. Nevertheless, more and more men and women believed in the Lord and were added to their number. As a result, people brought the sick into the streets and laid them on beds and mats so that at least Peter's shadow might fall on some of them as he passed by. Crowds gathered also from the towns around Jerusalem, bringing their sick and those tormented by impure spirits, and all of them were healed.[4]

There it is again. Salvation and signs and wonders among the people. People living out the miraculous and people led to faith. None of it happened in a building. All of it occurred among the people.

This is also how the angel of the Lord directed the apostles to continue the ministry of Jesus:

> During the night an angel of the Lord opened the doors of the jail and brought them out. "Go, stand

in the temple courts," he said, "and tell the people all about this new life."[5]

Notice the angel didn't release them back to the safety of the church. Instead it sent them back onto the streets. Heaven isn't intent on making church a safe place. Heaven is intent on unlocking the destiny of the city. God's goal is not our safety but our city. And so the angel instructed the apostles to go stand among the people and bring life. Don't worry about preserving the church or promoting the church. Instead proclaim the kingdom among the people and watch them come alive.

Our leadership team hadn't heard an angel, but we had heard from heaven. "If you will go after the lost, I will build the church." I had missed that statement in the church-planting manual. So I spent years trying to build the church. It never crossed my mind that my efforts might hinder the kingdom. Jesus didn't ask me or want me (or any other leader) to build His church. He said *He* would build His church.

The church Jesus builds is not an institution; His church is a movement. It is a movement of sent people who bring life to cities. The movement flourishes through the risky actions of scattered servants. It is what happens in the lives of these scattered servants that inscribes the story of hope in cities and industries, families and communities.

Unleashing the movement requires relinquishing our ownership of His church. It is His task to build the church; our task is to introduce the King and His kingdom. We don't advance the kingdom—it is already advancing. Instead, we announce the kingdom, drawing attention to what God is already doing beyond the building, among the people.

God has already graced the city; God has already moved hearts. Therefore, we are not praying for more—for more love or more power—we are praying for a movement of people. The problem isn't that we don't have enough; the problem is that we haven't given what we have. Our problem isn't revival; our problem is release. We need to release a movement of people who stand in the city and shepherd the city into life.

Scattered Sheep Need Scattered Shepherds

The first mention of shepherds in the Gospels is in relation to broken cities, not growing churches:

> Jesus went through all the towns and villages, teaching in their synagogues, proclaiming the good news of the kingdom and healing every disease and sickness. When he saw the crowds, he had compassion on them, because they were harassed and helpless, like sheep without a shepherd.... Then he said to his disciples, "The harvest is plentiful but the workers are few. Ask the Lord of the harvest, therefore, to send out workers into his harvest field."[6]

The shepherd doesn't stay in the building. The shepherd goes to the field. So today Jesus sends His shepherds into every aspect of society to meet scattered sheep. Only scattered shepherds can bring back life to scattered sheep. While we wait for greater anointing in the church, we miss our appointment in the field.

God has an *appointment* for you in your field. God has an *anointing* for you in your field. God has an assignment for you to release the destiny of others. This is the purpose of divine authority—to release others—individuals and institutions into their destiny.

Survival is too low a goal.

Revival is too low a goal.

The glorious goal is bringing life to every city. The King and His kingdom revealed and released to every hurting heart. Everyone, everywhere can come alive to the glory and story of God. So the Father of All Compassion scatters His servants to bring healing, hope, and honor among the people.

The Kingdom Comes as We Go

In the book of Acts, we are introduced to Stephen, a man full of God's grace and power who performed great wonders and signs among the people.[7] Yet long before Stephen demonstrated the kingdom in this way, the psalmist prophesied and declared it to be so: "You are the God who performs miracles; you display your power among the peoples."[8] He displays His power as His people "declare his glory among the nations, his marvelous deeds among all peoples."[9] In every generation, throughout church history, God has sent His people among the people to display His power.

The famous preacher John Wesley, unable to gather a congregation in a building, traveled throughout the English countryside declaring the gospel among the people. He was known as a field preacher rather than a church preacher. As he preached in the fields, Wesley stumbled upon a kingdom truth: when the church turns its face outward, the kingdom comes in power.[10]

While Wesley stumbled onto the truth, Scottish evangelist John Govan actively pursued it, perhaps inspired by Wesley and most definitely by his contemporary George Whitfield. He longed to see vast numbers of his countrymen encounter Christ. He wrote: "At that time the Lord put a longing in my heart that I might be endued with great power for service. I had some power in speaking but not what the disciples had."[11]

He continued to pray until breakthrough came. Once it did, he said, "I am not at all satisfied yet with what I know about this gift of the Holy Ghost. I want a far deeper experience and to see signs following."[12]

John Govan realized it wasn't going to happen in the building. He began to gather a missional movement that would enter the community. Initially these scattered servants weren't at all convinced of their identity or authority. They were deeply aware of their vulnerability but knew the message was one of expansive hope. And so they moved out in faith. By the end of the first year, "the Faith Mission" throughout the nation of Scotland witnessed two thousand people surrender their lives to Christ. Soon the mission spread in vision, persecution, and power until multiple thousands in multiple nations were captivated by the King and His kingdom.

The kingdom comes as we go!

We have spent so long praying for revival in the church that we have missed what God is doing in the world. We wait for God to fill us, oblivious to His invitation to show up among the people. In essence, God is saying, "If you give what I have already given you to the lost, the lowest, and the least, I will give you more. If you take what is in your hands and share, I will ensure you never go empty."

I discovered this for the first time on a mission trip to South Africa in 2004. Our team was invited to serve in the community of Hillbrow, Johannesburg. We had never heard of Hillbrow so didn't consider that it might be dangerous territory. Yet as our hosts talked us through the evening, we had a growing sense of concern, particularly as they said, "You should take off your jewelry and kiss your wives good-bye."

We laughed, thinking they were joking. Their faces told us they were not.

I became increasingly nervous about leading a team of eight people into a community where, on average, several people were raped and one person was murdered daily. This was not how I had imagined the trip, nor how I wanted to be remembered within the Vineyard movement. Alan Scott, the guy who led his people to martyrdom!

My concerns heightened when we met our host for the evening.

He introduced himself, saying, "Hi, my name is Sicko."

Sicko had an eight-foot cross and a bucket of water for washing people's feet. His plan was to carry the cross through the community. Somehow neither of these symbols felt reassuring or comforting. I was wrestling to control the growing voice inside my head declaring we were all doomed!

After mustering sufficient faith, we got in the van and set off.

As night fell, there we were standing in Hillbrow, one of the roughest parts of Johannesburg, inviting God to show up and do what He alone can do among spiritually lost people. Our initial conversations made us feel anxious. It never did get easier. Yet by the end of the evening, eight people had said yes to God for the first time and taken the next step on their spiritual journey.

Hope had come to Hillbrow.

Truthfully, hope had been there all along.

Hidden hope was manifest as the church showed up.

One outstanding moment involved praying for a chemically dependent young man who had a hole in his leg. Initially as our team prayed, nothing happened. Refusing to take no for an answer, we prayed a second time—again nothing happened. We prayed Pentecostal prayers, Baptist prayers, Catholic prayers, every prayer imaginable. Still nothing. Then one of our pastors took hold of the young man's feet and washed them. As he did, the young man indicated all pain left, his leg was healed, and then the wound closed in front of our eyes. We were all amazed.

That night in Hillbrow, we entered the city empty and came back full. It would be one of many such occasions.

Something incredible happens when the church moves into the community and demonstrates the kingdom with compassion and authority, among people who secretly hope that life change is possible and who are secretly hoping that God is available to them. All too often, we stay in gathered environments counting the numbers of people who attend. Yet God beckons us to live courageously as scattered servants exploring just how far His kingdom reaches as we give it away. He invites us to discover that ministry works among people outside the church, because He is at work outside the church.

Spiritually lost people are irresistible to the Spirit of God. They are at the heart of the mission of Jesus and the longing of the Father. Therefore, every step scattered servants take beyond the building is a step into what God is doing. And every time we do, we can almost hear the whisper of the Father say, "You are My children and I have given you good things to share. As you follow Me, you will encounter people who are far from Me, who are fighting for faith, struggling in their marriages, longing for healing, wondering if I am alive. As you meet them, share what I give you for them. Don't worry if it feels like you have nothing to offer. It is My pleasure to send you out empty but bring you back full."

Indeed, the kingdom always comes as the church goes.

Chapter 3

THE MIND-SET
THAT BRINGS LIFE

The dream of God over your life is not that you become a believer and help out the local church. The dream of God over your life is that you come alive in His presence and bring life to every environment, spilling contagious hope into hurting humanity. God has entrusted believers with an assignment to lead the earth into life.

When God created humanity, He called it to shape the world. Man's first moments were filled with breath-giving honor. Adam knew he was not only treasured, he was trusted. He was placed at the center of culture and invited to create from a place of intimate connection. The one who had received life was now charged with bringing life ... trusted to create and to cultivate.

So Adam began declaring the nature of that which surrounded him.[1] He did so in an atmosphere of the Father's delight. Adam knew he was entrusted to rule—trusted to be a culture carrier—one who would shape culture through ideas, inventions, and innovations harnessed to the beauty and majesty of God.

Exceptional Trust

Remarkably, the biblical story and the human story begin with God entrusting humanity to lead the earth into life:

> God said, "Let Us make man in Our image, according to Our likeness; let them have dominion over the fish of the sea, over the birds of the air, and over the cattle, over all the earth and over every creeping thing that creeps on the earth." So God created man in His own image; in the image of God He created him; male and female He created them. Then God blessed them, and God said to them, "Be fruitful and multiply; fill the earth and subdue it; have dominion over the fish of the sea, over the birds of the air, and over every living thing that moves on the earth."[2]

Human beings were trusted to rule and bring design. They were trusted to speak words and live lives that shape culture.

It's awesome. It's awkward.

To be human is to be … trusted.

God knows it's only in an environment of trust that we come fully alive and bring life to every environment. This "bringing-life-to-every-environment" is the task, the joy, the glory of humanity made in the image of God.

Consider again the words, "Let them reign...." These are words pregnant with permission. Such vulnerability displayed by divinity. Such authority entrusted to humanity.

In this formative, expansive, creative moment, the living God, the God who gives life, reveals both His incredible love and His exceptional trust.

Believers often have a difficulty believing God trusts them. Many know from bitter experience that the heart is deceitful above all things. Therefore, it's difficult to conceive that God would trust His people. Love them? Yes! Trust them? No! Since we don't trust ourselves, we assume God doesn't trust us.

Yet Scripture makes it clear that God loves us, and love always trusts.[3] The covenants (old and new) imply and impart trust. Reluctantly or willingly, we find ourselves in a trust-filled relationship. This expansive trust-filled relationship is held together by honor rather than rules. Think of it. God trusts you so much, He moved in with you.

You are not only loved, you are trusted.

You are not only treasured, you are trusted.

As the story of humanity has unfolded, there have been moments divine trust was regretted. God was grieved that He had made man, that man had abused trust, creativity, and authority, that man operated outside of connection, outside of glory.[4] All sinned and fell short of the glory, the original design.[5]

But while divine trust was regretted, it was never rescinded. Man continued to live with authority to shape culture. He continued to live with the capacity for creating and reigning—although mankind frequently continued to abuse his authority, to abandon his humanity, to abdicate his glory. Nonetheless, man remained crowned with glory and honor.[6]

He may have been *enslaved* by others, but he remained *entrusted* by the Father.

Extraordinary Authority

There is more to the Creation narrative than exceptional trust. We discover that to be human is also to have extraordinary authority. In the beginning, authority was given to humanity. We don't get far in the story before discovering the exceptional power God has given to man, with authority to shape environments. "Rule and bring order"—that is what humanity does when it lives according to original design. We debase our humanity when we deny our authority. Rejoicing in the authority given to mankind, the psalmist exclaims, "You have made him to have dominion over the works of Your hands; You have put all things under his feet."[7]

All things? Every environment? Really?

It's astonishing authority. It's especially risky. It all sounds like too much, too far, more than mankind can handle.

And again the divine dream declares, "Lead the earth into life! Your destiny is to release the design of others. Your assignment is to bring life." God allows humanity the opportunity to thrive in a place of honor and glory, furnishing humanity with the responsibility to bring life to every environment.

It's daunting, even unnerving. So daunting that invariably we retreat to the position of reluctant rulers. We would rather be volunteers in His church than participants in His story. Yet we have been given authority.

Authority to restrain evil and release good.

Authority that causes the earth to come alive.

Authority in all things.

It's awesome. It's awkward.

To be human is to … rule and reign over all things.

We have settled for building churches, rather than using our authority to bring life to cities. And yet Jesus was exceptionally clear: "I will build My church; you have the keys of the kingdom"—in effect He invites us to take the keys of our authority into the community and introduce it to its divine destiny.[8]

King David understood this reality. As Israel's king, he knew he had authority to awaken a nation to its God-given destiny. He understood that he was a trusted ruler. Although *he* was royalty, his song of trust recorded in Psalm 8 makes it clear that he knew the Spirit rested on *all* humanity with glorious honor.

In the New Testament, Peter phrased it this way: "But you are a chosen people, a royal priesthood, a holy nation, God's special possession, that you may declare the praises of him who called you out of darkness into his wonderful light."[9] Our capacity to bring honor to God in the world never exceeds our understanding of our *royal* identity.

You are carrying kingdom authority, and whenever you awaken to that authority, it changes you and everyone around you. You can never enter an environment you don't have authority in. So you never have to fight for authority. There is never a room you're in that you don't have authority in it, except when you surrender your authority at the door. Every time you surrender your authority, you lose some of your identity.

Royal Priesthood

Only royalty has authority to bring back life to nations. It's the task of rulers to lead the earth into life. Kings, of course, have a royal identity. They have a responsibility. And kings understand it's their responsibility to supply the destiny of a whole nation. That's what kings exist to do. They rule and reign, demonstrating authority in a way that releases humanity. It's who kings are.

Therefore, when the Bible calls us a *royal* priesthood, it invites us to recognize our identity, that we are adopted sons and daughters of the living God. Next, we understand our God-given responsibility to supply the destiny of nations. Kings learn to operate as trusted rulers in every environment. Obviously when God calls us royalty, He's not sharing His sovereignty with us. It doesn't in any way diminish who He is, but rather it demonstrates what He is choosing to do in releasing His sovereignty through us. Theologian N. T. Wright says:

> You are called to a throne…. The wise rule of humans over creation (the earth) is what being made in God's image is partly all about. The image does not refer principally to some aspect of human nature or character which is especially like God. As many writers have shown, it points to the belief that just as ancient rulers might place statues of themselves in far-flung cities to remind subject

peoples who was ruling them, so God has placed His own Image, human being into this world, so that the world can see who its ruler is. Not only see, but experience. Precisely because God is the God of generous, creative, overflowing love, his way of running things is to share power, to work through his image bearers, to invite their free and glad collaboration.[10]

Just as it is unthinkable that God would not be creative and expansive, it is equally inconceivable that He wouldn't operate in partnership. Paul picks this up in his letter to the Romans when he writes, "We know that in all things God works together with those he loves to release what is good."[11] We wait on God to do things for us, but God wants to do things with us.

Jesus once had a conversation with His closest followers when they asked Him, "Lord, are You going to at this time restore the kingdom to Israel?" They had forgotten what Jesus had already spoken to them: "I confer on you a kingdom, just as my Father conferred one on me."[12] Essentially, He said, "I am not *restoring* the kingdom at this time; I am *releasing* the kingdom at this time. And I am going to do it through you and with you. Everyday. Everywhere. Each of you will receive power to partner so that you can renew everything everywhere. It will require relentless prayer and relentless patience, but I am calling each of you to release the kingdom that you're waiting for Me to release over you. You are a royal priesthood, and My gift to the world is you."

We are His royal priesthood, and His gift to the world is us.

Crowned with Glory and Honor

All of this is heady stuff. Yet if we are to become life giving to people and places around us, we must allow the Lord to honor and affirm us as His children without fearing pride. Jesus said, "My Father will honor the one who serves me."[13] God has seated us in a place of honor. Yet often we are reluctant and desperately uncomfortable because we don't know what to do with divine honor.

We are rightly uncomfortable with honoring ourselves, but this is receiving the Father's gift over us. No one should seek his own honor, but no one should disown the honor of the Father. We are so afraid of pride, but there is a difference between becoming puffed up and being raised up.

In John 13, Peter struggled with the idea of King Jesus washing his feet, but Jesus apparently didn't have a problem with it.[14] Peter struggled to sit at the table while God honored him, yet Jesus is not insecure. He is not afraid to exalt us.

It's awesome. It's awkward.

To be human is to be … honored.

We were made to be crowned with honor … and glory.

The idea of glory sits uncomfortably with us. We are happy to sing, "In my life, Lord, be glorified," but we struggle when God makes His glory visible in us and on us. However, scattered servants think differently. They know that God loves to reveal His glory in their lives.

False humility lives afraid of glory. True humility carries glory.

Often we pray, "Less of me and more of You," or "All of You, none of me." But God doesn't want it to be all Him and none of you. He had *that* before He created you. Yet in love, He chose you because He wants it to be ALL of Him in ALL of you. His greatness is never dependent on making you less. It is demonstrated in raising you up with Christ.

"And God raised us up with Christ and seated us with him in the heavenly realms in Christ Jesus, in order that in the coming ages he might show the incomparable riches of his grace, expressed in his kindness to us in Christ Jesus."[15]

We do not proclaim God's sovereignty by devaluing our humanity. He invites us to be image bearers, and image bearers of the most glorious God are always filled with glory. The sovereignty of God is not a *substitute* for the glory of man. It is the *source* of the glory of man. His desire is that our lives become a reference point for His glory. And sometimes God does stuff to make us look good.[16]

Step Into Your Royal Identity

We meet Gideon in the Old Testament book of Judges while he is threshing wheat in a winepress.[17] God said, essentially, "Hey, mighty warrior." He didn't say, "Hey, don't think too highly of yourself! Don't be thinking you're more than you are. Don't even entertain the idea that you actually carry a solution for the nations. Always remember it's Me." No! He says, "Hello, mighty warrior." By the end of the story, Gideon steps into his identity. He emerges as a mighty warrior. He becomes what God named and graced him to be all along.

Then there is Saul, the first king of Israel. He wore the symbols of glory and honor but missed the reality of it in his own life. Saul was an insecure, broken individual who hadn't quite captured his true royalty. He suddenly became king, but he didn't know who he was. It's always a dangerous thing to have authority without identity. Sadly, Saul lived in that reality, yet when he came across the company of the prophets, they declared, "Whatever your hand finds to do, just go ahead and do it. The Lord is on you."[18]

Really? Whatever your hand finds to do? Yes, the Lord's heart is with you and His hand is on you. He likes you. He's for you.

If a man in the Old Testament who was insecure and impoverished in his identity received that level of authority when the Holy Spirit came upon him, how much more in the New Testament when the Spirit indwells us? Are we given that level of freedom and authority? Expansively more, immeasurable more—and yet we're still afraid. We're afraid of overstretching the boundaries. We are afraid because we have forgotten we are crowned with glory and honor. And the crown does not sit easily on us.

Nevertheless, Jesus *has* conferred on us a kingdom. As ambassadors of the kingdom, we already have what we need. We don't need to pray, asking God to make us less. He wants to show us off. "You are the light of the world. A town built on a hill cannot be hidden."[19] He says, "Stop thinking it's holy to hide—get visible. You are the light of the world, and unless you show up, people never see it. Unless you show up in your true identity, then the world never comes into its true identity."

Instead of praying, "Less of me and more of You," try praying: "God, make my life a reference point for Your grace and glory. God, when You're moving on the earth, let it be known that You're moving through me."

As scattered servants, we say, "The God who moved in the pages of the Old Testament and New Testament, this is my God. He shows up in my life. He does amazing things in my life. I have the same access, the same privilege as those saints of old. I am called to demonstrate the same incredible power, the same outrageous compassion, the same exceptional trust, the same extraordinary authority." Because …

To be human is to be His.

Chapter 4

CHANGING THE CULTURE ONE LIFE AT A TIME

A stunned silence filled the room.

Looking back, it was crazy. I stood before our congregation and announced we were committing to the goal of seeing one hundred people say *yes* to God for the first time that year. But in the history of Causeway Coast Vineyard Church, we hadn't seen ten people come to Christ. Searching for solace after the service, I said to Kathryn, "What have we done? Everyone will be so discouraged when no one comes to faith." She smiled and nodded in a way that communicated, "That was pretty dumb."

Nonetheless, we had a plan.

Our big plan was to have everyone write down the names of friends or family with whom they had shared their story and for whom they would like us to pray. We would pray together and invite God to change lives. So we prayed and waited.

Much to our surprise, a few days later the first person gave his life to God. We shared the story the following Sunday. A couple of weeks later, it happened again. Now the sense of energy and momentum was becoming palpable.

More people brought their friends, who brought their friends, who began opening their lives to God. Something was shifting. Instead of gathering each Sunday to get a story *for* the week, we gathered to share our stories *from* the week.

By the end of that year, 104 people had come to faith. We were off and running, chasing the expansive goodness of God and learning to bring life to our community one life at a time.

Believers Don't Do Evangelism

Believers don't do evangelism; believers bring life. Nowhere in Scripture is there a command to "do evangelism." There is, however, the promise of a generous, expansive life. Believers enter the divine life, steeping their hearts in God initiatives and God provisions, and then carry His life into their culture.[1] Believers don't do evangelism; believers bring life.

It's amazing the lengths Jesus will go to in order to bring life to spiritually lost people. Remember the boat trip where He endangered His friends' lives so He could reach one man who was alone, afraid, and far from God?

Remember the diversion through Samaria for the sake of one spiritually confused woman? These are helpful paradigms. They remind us that when we pursue God, He deliberately disrupts our comfort, our normal life patterns, our usual relationships, and leads us to lay down our lives to bring life to people who are far from God.

In our local church, we were seeking to help people join God in what He was doing in our community. We wanted to create a pathway that would help us become the kind of people who lived with the *whole* world on our hearts, not just the church world. We knew that most believers want to bring life to the city, but they don't know how to bring life to the city. It seems overwhelming.

As we scanned Scripture, we stumbled upon a pathway that helped people identify a next step they could take in pursuing God as He pursues the lost. Rooted in the gospel of John, chapter 4, the pathway was simple, and it's the one we still use today. I encourage you to read the story in that chapter about Jesus' interaction with the woman at the well in Samaria. It is a tender account and a model for reaching people with the gospel. Borrowing a term I first heard used by Andy Stanley, we call this path "Invest and Invite."

Initiate Contact with Non-Christians

The first part of the personal pathway is initiating contact with non-Christians, people God is calling and drawing to Himself. These individuals (like the Samaritan woman) are God-seekers and God-fearers even though they often don't look like it because of their baggage. People who are looking for God don't always look like they are looking for God.

Two lads from our church were in a local bar when they were approached by two young ladies. Both ladies had recently been released from a local psychiatric unit. As they entered the bar, they mentioned that all they wanted to do that evening was get exceptionally drunk and have sex. "Is that all you want from this evening?" asked one of the young men, James. Thinking he might oblige, they said yes.

James asked if they would like to know what he was doing with his evening. He told them he was seeking to invite people into hope and life. One of the girls listened intently as James' friend Dave shared his hope. She asked them to escort her outside while she had a smoke. There, she asked to hear more about Jesus and our church. The next week, she attended our Alpha class and one of our Sunday services. She thought she was looking for intoxication and sex, but she was really looking for God.

I also recall a young woman named Jessica, who sat in class listening as her teacher explained the folly of maintaining belief in God. But Jessica had been captivated by the beauty of God, who had healed the scars of abandonment, abuse, and self-harm in her life. It was impossible for her to agree with the teacher, so she tentatively raised her hand in full awareness that a public confrontation would ensue.

The two debated for a while before eventually Jessica was rescued by the school bell. She arrived at her classroom early the next morning. The teacher was waiting. Jessica anticipated further conflict but was stunned as the teacher pulled her aside to tell her that the previous evening he and his partner had given their lives to Christ.

People who are looking for God don't always look like they are looking for God.

The Samaritan woman who encountered Jesus at the well looked like she was conducting her business for the day. She seemed disinterested in faith. But even though she didn't look like she was looking for God, God was searching for her. Jesus made sure He connected with her, intentionally starting the conversation. Likewise, if we are going to bring life to our city, we must fight the inward drift of our lives and intentionally say, "God, disrupt my life in a way that leads me to the lost. Introduce me to people who live on the other side." It's a prayer God will always answer.

One of my friends, Martin, was asking God to help him connect with unbelievers who were recent migrants to his country. As he prayed, he sensed the prompting of the Holy Spirit to go to a certain district in the city. Upon arriving, he saw several people of African descent. He sensed these were the people the Lord had highlighted to him, so he took the initiative and he said hello.

After introducing himself, he engaged in a brief conversation before inviting them to attend his church the next day. They politely declined, explaining they couldn't afford the bus fare. In a moment of insight and generosity, Martin offered to reimburse their expenses and feed them if they attended the service.

The next morning, Martin waited patiently and prayerfully for their arrival. Instead of the seven or eight people he had expected, sixteen people arrived. After reimbursing their expenses and providing food, Martin invited them to continue to explore the life of Jesus through engaging in community.

Over time, two small groups formed, soon growing and multiplying. Then even more multiplication occurred. Together these people thought it would be wonderful to plant and support churches back in their homeland. Today there are dozens of congregations in the Democratic Republic of the Congo and in other parts of Africa that have been planted as a result of their ministry. It's an incredible story. Yet nothing would have happened unless Martin had gone out of his way to initiate contact.

This is exactly what Jesus did with the Samaritan woman. He seized the initiative in speaking with her. Everything that happened thereafter was a consequence of that conversation. Each meaningful connection starts with hello. It starts with a handshake, an introduction, or, as Bill Hybels says, "a walk across the room." If you will do that, here's what will happen: your palms will sweat and your throat will go dry. But as Joyce Meyer wonderfully says, when that happens, "lick your palms and get on with it."

Involve Unbelievers in Your Life

The second step in the process of bringing life to your community is becoming more involved with unbelievers. We don't have to look far to engage with spiritually lost people. Our workplaces are filled with people who are hurting and longing for change in their lives. These are people desperate to break free from the only life they have ever known and break into the only life they ever wanted. These are people carrying secrets, yearning for something and someone real. In His wisdom, God has strategically positioned you so you can influence them. Involve them in your life.

For some believers, that can be a scary thought. Some fear they will start drifting from God themselves. Yet Jesus never feared being contaminated by the Samaritan woman. Instead, He engaged her in conversation, expecting that what rested on His life was going to change her life. His presence would make all the difference in her circumstance. We need to cultivate a similar awareness of the contagious power of holiness on our lives and stop excluding people God is longing to include.

While some of us fear losing our faith, I suspect others struggle to involve unbelievers in their lives for a very different reason. *We are not afraid of becoming like them; we are afraid of letting them see the real us.* We are painfully aware of our weaknesses, our imperfections, and our failures. We wonder, *How can I talk about the night-and-day difference Christ makes in a life when at times my own life is a mess?* So here's what we tend to do … We work on sorting our life before we share it. And of course our lives are never really sorted. And that's okay. It's more than okay. It's divine design.

We have this treasure in jars of clay.

Our communities are drawn to brokenness more than excellence. We try to impress them with our brilliance, but our brokenness and imperfection are our greatest gifts. Focus on sharing your life before you sort it. You don't need to have it all together before you give it all away. Indeed, you won't find the life you are looking for until you start to share the life you have.[2]

You can't sell something that is broken. But as believers, we have nothing to sell and everything to share. And you can't share something until it's broken. People around us need our brokenness as much as our wholeness. People in your industry, family, and community have become so scarred by life that they are desperate to know if it's possible to recover. If you have a neat, sanitized life, they are never going to ask you to explain where your hope comes from. They'll never ask how you deal with stress, unforgiveness, and debt. However, if you vulnerably open up your pain and with integrity open up your past, they will see

63

there is hope. They will start asking, "How did you recover? How are you recovering? What is the source of your hope?"

As Peter told us, "You need to be prepared to give an answer to everyone who asks you to give the reason for the hope you have." I grew up in a tradition that regarded this verse as functioning primarily in regard to apologetics. We thought it meant, *Make sure you have all the answers so you can defend the faith.* While that's legitimate and helpful in certain contexts, it's not what the apostle Peter intended. Peter was writing to a community that was suffering and struggling, but the way they handled their hearts was evoking a response from a watching world. Their commitment to persistence in the midst of pain was the talk of the town.

It's the same today. Your non-Christian friends and family are looking at your life, wondering what you have and how you have it. It's time for you to give the reason for the hope that is in you. Make the decision to courageously, vulnerably, and authentically share your needs and dreams with unbelievers. Involve them in your life.

Investing through Prayer and Fasting

Don't stop there. Invest in people's lives through prayer and fasting. It is my conviction that Jesus was praying for the Samaritan woman as He spoke with her. He was seeking insight into her life, depending on the Holy Spirit to turn up. We have the responsibility and opportunity to do the same.

I have come to share the conviction of Rick Warren when he says, "I believe that anybody can be won to Christ if you just discover the key to his/her heart. Start praying to partner, 'Lord, help me to see what's the key to their heart.' It may be a problem with their kids. It may be loneliness. It may be a bankruptcy or unemployment. It may be stress on the job. It may be a question about a friend who died. It may be that they are addicted or self-harming. Everybody has a hidden hurt. Count on it. Everybody."[3]

Everybody Has a Hidden Hurt

I know a young woman named Michelle, who was in a coffee shop with friends when she noticed a couple sitting at one of the tables. She sensed God wanted her to meet with them. But it felt awkward because they were engaged in conversation.

Michelle sensed they had financial difficulties and would be declared bankrupt if circumstances didn't change by Christmas. She looked at them again, acutely aware that nothing on the outside indicated their need. They were sharply dressed and looked comparatively wealthy. She continued to pray and, as she did, became convinced that this was their hidden hurt.

So boldly she approached the couple, apologized for interrupting their conversation, and explained she was a student learning to bring encouragement to people. She told them she sensed that they were in financial difficulty. As she spoke, the gentleman could not look at her and the lady couldn't take her eyes off her. When she finished, the lady recounted their story. They were financially drowning and had made the decision that morning to declare themselves bankrupt if nothing changed by Christmas.

Michelle prayed for the couple and recommended Christians Against Poverty as a way of tackling debt in their lives. As far as I am aware, they have not yet given their lives to Christ, but they are absolutely aware of God's care for them. Everybody has a hidden hurt. Everyone has things in their heart that only the Father knows.

As for the Samaritan woman, she was sexually broken. I'm not sure whether Jesus knew that at the beginning of the conversation, but at some point the Father revealed her hidden hurt. *She has had five husbands and the man she now lives with is not her husband.*

When you ask God to show you what is troubling your friend, family member, work colleague, or neighbor, He has committed to speaking to you. "Call to me and I will answer you and tell you great and unsearchable things you do not know."[4] There are things He knows about your colleagues and neighbors that He is waiting to share with you.

Invest in the people around you through prayer and fasting. Start today. Write down the names of two people who you know are far from God and commit to praying for them. You don't have to be good at praying for a long time. You can pray daily for a short time. Pray, asking God to show you what is keeping these people from Him. Don't rely on what you think is keeping them from Him, or even what they have told you is keeping them from Him. Instead, ask God to show you the secrets of their hearts, and He will make them known to you. And then pray!

As you pray, these people will begin to be drawn to God. They will become convinced, by your life, that following Christ is genuinely a better way to live. It's a better way to stay married, to raise kids, to handle finance, to construct relationships, to engage influence, to demonstrate compassion, to work creatively, an all-round better way to live.

Invite Them to a Place of Encounter

When the people you are reaching out to look for more, invite them to a place of encounter where they can experience Christ themselves. This is what the Samaritan woman did in her town. She invited friends, family, neighbors, and enemies to come and see! Come and encounter![5]

Encounters often happen in life-giving, life-transforming environments. Our Easter service is one of those environments. Last year we interviewed our friend Amanda as part of the lead-in to Easter. She told how her friendship with Kathryn began at the school gates many years before and how they became involved in each other's lives. As the friendship grew, Kathryn invited her to one of our Easter services in 2012. She decided to come with her family, and although she wasn't quite ready to publicly respond to Christ, He won her heart from that moment.

As we interviewed her, she told the story of attending church every week in the year that followed, until she gave her heart to Jesus, along with her three children. Then she told of her baptism and how her husband, Peter, stood alongside her in the water. He was not yet a believer but was undone as she was baptized. It was less than a year later that he gave his yes to Jesus too.

We asked Peter and their girls to come and join us on the stage. Amanda went on to tell us about the friends she had invited to church, even before she had come to faith herself. One of those friends had brought her husband along, and both gave their lives to Jesus within a few weeks of attending. We invited them to come and join us on the stage too.

Then Amanda told us of another family with the same story, so we invited them to come and join us on the stage as well.

One by one, each of those friends, along with their families, came and told the story of what Jesus had done in their lives through their connection with Amanda, until at the end of that interview, there were eighteen people sitting on the stage—eighteen lives transformed.

Amanda doesn't have the gift of evangelism, but she does know how to bring life. She and her family are so grateful Kathryn invited her to that service long ago.

Imagine

You have probably heard of studies showing that 25 percent of people will come to church if a friend invites them. Make the invite. In 2004 and 2005, as we were working this through in our local church, I shared the following:

> Imagine if one out of every four of your friends or people in your school started moving closer to God. Imagine what our church would look like if people were ablaze with a passion for God and a passion for the lost. Imagine people turning up early so they could pray for spiritually distant friends and family. Imagine worship where hunger is overwhelming because we need God to come for the sake of His glory and the sake of His kingdom, because people we love are perishing without God and without

hope in the world. Imagine the welcome we would give to newcomers because of the effort it's taken to bring them here. Imagine we didn't just look upon them as new young people, or more young people, but as the answer to the cry of our heart and the cry of heaven. Imagine how eager we would be to receive from God's Word because we want to share the bread of life with a dying generation. I think it would revolutionize Sundays at the very least for us. It may take us some time to get there, but that's where we are going because that is in part what a vibrant, missional community looks like.

Fast-forward a few years, and this time the room is a little larger. There is no stunned silence now, only the sound of resounding applause and anticipation. It had been ten years since that first announcement. I had just told our congregation we were believing God to bring life to fifteen hundred people this year.

So far we have seen two thousand two hundred and fifty-seven.

Chapter 5

REPOSITIONING THE CHURCH TO REACH THE LOST

His eyes conveyed the yearning in his heart. The intensity in his voice increased as he described the tension of wrestling with developing an outward-focused church.

Yet another young leader, yearning for greater evangelistic potency in his community, inwardly longing for an expansive heart to grip his church so they could move from being introspective to becoming expansive with their faith. His recent church plant had already gathered hundreds of people. Yet he had that familiar look in his eyes. I had seen that look before. I remembered those unspoken words:

"This isn't going to be enough for me."

"I don't simply want to put on better services."

"I don't want to be the new trendy church for disillusioned believers."

"I don't want to create a culture of consumers."

"I don't just want to 'brand' what we do. I want the presence and power of God to mark us and everything we do."

Later that day, I met another millennial leader. He wasn't a church planter; he was a seasoned minister wrestling with a church in transition. He spent his days waiting for the moment that would fuel movement. Yet it never happened, and the questions haunted him.

"What do we need to do? What structure will create turnaround?"

He was unaware his questions revealed a mind-set that sabotaged the culture he was seeking to create. His theory was sound ... get my church right, create better environments, people will bring their friends, and sooner or later things will change. Sadly, they won't.

This pastor loved his church. He didn't yet love his city enough to upset his church.

In another continent, I sat with an empowered leader experiencing remarkable miracles, signs, and wonders. In their context, it is common for God to show up on the streets. Their Sunday services are marked with an exceptional sense of God's presence. On the surface, he had everything the heart could ever want. Underneath, he was haunted by the lack of people coming to faith.

"This isn't going to be enough for me."

"I want more than renewal."

"I want more than the supernatural in our services."

"I want more than healed bodies."

"I want changed communities."

And then the recurring questions came:

"Is it possible to see lots of people come to faith in our services *and* actively welcome the empowering ministry of the Holy Spirit? Am I expecting too much? How do we move beyond brilliant services to changed communities? How do we get everyone involved in leading the city into life? How do we create and sustain supernatural missional culture?"

The good news is it's possible. The bad news is it's painful.

Creating Environments That Lead Lost People into Life

If we are to reach our cities, we must reposition our churches. It's easier to attend a church that gathers lost people than become a people who alter communities. Yet God is not sending lost people into the church; He sends the church out into the world. Our cities long for life, and to reach them we have to reposition our churches.

Jesus illustrated what loving the city looks like. As civic and religious leaders questioned His associations and motivations, He told three stories depicting the relentlessly missional nature of God.[1]

Just like the woman in Luke 15 turning the house inside out and upside down searching for the lost coin.[2] The scene is one of intentional disruption for the purpose of finding what is missing. Everything within the house is subject to being repositioned until the owner's treasure is found. In the same way, church leaders have to risk upsetting people to reset the priorities.

As Andy Stanley points out, the sense of tension is not new. *Many of the big fights recorded in the book of Acts relate to the tension the church faced as she wrestled with the nature of the community she was becoming.*[3] Until then, the church had grown without being hospitable to those on the outside. But at this critical moment in the history of the faith community, they gathered to listen to one another and to the Holy Spirit. They came to an inescapable conclusion and an irreversible momentum....

We should not make it difficult for the Gentiles who are turning to God.[4]

They were redrawing their relationship circle. They were making a commitment together for the sake of others. They were saying, "Whatever else we do, we need to stay open *and* outward. Let's be inclusive and expansive with our lives. Let's keep hospitality *and* generosity at the core. Let's avoid the tendency to drift inward. Let's let outsiders *in*."

Letting Outsiders In: Welcoming the Lost

Like those first disciples, we have been prompted and commanded to remain inclusive and expansive. We are called to "not make it difficult for those who are turning to God." We must find ways of creating gathered environments that prioritize lost people and embrace the value of letting outsiders in.

Faced with this reality at Causeway Coast Vineyard, we began to repent—literally to change our thoughts—about inviting outsiders. We never meant it to be difficult; we just had never really thought about it. So from April 2003 to April 2005, we did think about it. A LOT! We examined every aspect of our services and our lifestyles and reordered them to include outsiders. All of our services and all of our energies were redesigned with our guests in mind. For the first time, we intentionally created environments that engaged with spiritually lost people—environments where people who were far from God could encounter Him without unnecessary obstacles.[5]

Creating Intentional Accessible Environments

The change I am describing involved significant restructuring of our Sunday services. Here is a glimpse of what that looked like:

Welcome and Worship

- We started on time (rather unusual for a Vineyard church)
- We started to call visitors "guests" and focused on welcoming them
- We didn't change our emphasis or style of worship, but we altered the length of worship from forty minutes to approximately twenty-five minutes

Announcements

- We featured announcements more likely to captivate guests and announced sermon series in a creative way, weeks in advance
- We had our people sign up on a sheet to invite other people to our next series

- We used this time to celebrate stories of people who were risking contact with non-Christians without results
- We occasionally used this time to pray for all the people with whom we were sharing our life and faith

Sermon

- We kept it simple
- We made it understandable for our guests
- We focused mainly on life application
- We usually introduced things by saying, "Sooner or later you will be speaking to a friend who is far from God, and that person will want to know how you ..."
- We had people share their stories as part of the sermon to illustrate one of the points, sometimes through video
- We always ended with an invitation to salvation, irrespective of the subject

Ministry/Response Time

- We started by helping non-Christians say yes to God
- We spent significantly less time at the front during ministry

- We learned to heal the sick quickly with a word
- We probably had "full-blown ministry" twice a month (where we invited people to the front for someone to pray with them)
- We explained to people that the gospel is the power of God, and where people are responding to the gospel, the power of God is at work
- We demystified the supernatural within the service and emphasized the supernatural beyond the building

None of this was particularly new or unique to us. Many churches operate with this model.[6] But it was a real shift for us. And while we were wrestling it through in our context, my friend David Parker shared this helpful analogy:

> Imagine you invited guests to your home for a meal. You would take time to inquire what your guests liked to eat. If they suggested something you didn't like, you would say you didn't like it and prepare something you both could enjoy. You would perhaps engage in extra preparation and cleaning that day, simply as a courtesy and honor to them.
>
> You would not show up for the meal in your boxer shorts, even though you may walk around your home in your boxers at other times. On these occasions you intentionally limit your freedom and your level of comfort simply because you have

guests. Similarly, while you may have a passionate marriage marked by physical intimacy, you would not demonstrate that passion during the meal; that would be wrong and rude. Your guests know that there are degrees of intimacy in your relationship and they are happy for you; they just don't want to be forced to watch.

His point was immediately obvious. If we are declaring our services open to all—and actively encouraging those in our churches to invite their friends—we must develop environments that engage insiders *and* outsiders. Our message (like Jesus' message) ought to have moments of connection, no matter where people are on their spiritual journey. And it is not only acceptable but deeply important that we limit certain practices to prioritize certain people.

We were convinced! So, rigorously adopting this approach, we became exceptional at reaching our community and engaging spiritually lost people. We saw multiples of people coming to faith. And the Lord added to our number monthly those who were being saved.

It was wonderful. It was everything we had longed and prayed for since we planted the church. It should have been enough. It wasn't.

The more broken people came to faith, the more we began to realize the upsurge in people coming to faith *wasn't changing us. It wasn't making us a missional people.* We still weren't taking the radical step beyond the building the Father's initial invitation had made available to us. It was clear that if we settled for people coming to know Jesus in our services, we were going to miss becoming the people the Lord had asked us to become. We were going to miss His promise—that if we would go after the lost, He would look after the church.

We had stopped making it difficult for people turning to God. We had redrawn our relationships. We now had gathered environments where people who were looking for God could attend. We had structures that leaned toward lost people, but we didn't yet have scattered servants—a movement of people empowered by the Holy Spirit and sent to bring life to the city. In His kindness, Jesus reminded us that our mandate was to GO.[7] We were prioritizing and finding the lost, yet insufficiently mobilizing the found.

We were not so much an Acts 2 community as we were a church becoming better at creating a friendly atmosphere. We lacked the dynamism of New Testament gatherings.[8] We were increasingly neglecting healing the sick and casting out demons. The Lord was asking us to get insiders out—*everyone* empowered so that they could carry the kingdom *everywhere*. He was asking us to move from a multiplication of gathered environments to a movement of sent people.

Getting Insiders Out: Unleashing the Church

It's become clear that hosting attractional services, where people come to faith regularly, is not the same as laying down our lives for Christ and the gospel. Attractional services are good but are insufficient to create and generate missional movement.[9] Without rigorous intentionality around mission, attractional services can become counterproductive to creating scattered servants. The number of people coming to faith gives us enough perceived "success" to inoculate the church from its responsibility to go. Like the early church, its effectiveness in people coming to faith locally can retard its missional mind-set.

In the Power of the Holy Spirit

I Corinthians 2:4
'Not with wise and persuasive words, but with a demonstration of the Spirit's power'

Let Outsiders In
Invites people to come IN

Acts 15:19
'We should not make it difficult for unbelievers'

GOAL

To reach a wide range of people and lead them into a God saved life

Attractional

Get Insiders Out
Invites people to GO OUT

Matthew 28:19
'Therefore GO and make disciples of all nations'

Missional

The church is both gathered *and* scattered.

We weren't called to simply create structures for church growth—adding more and more people. We were called to multiply, create, and sustain a missional culture—bringing more and more life to our city. God had spoken to us to GO after the lost, and we had certainly made some progress, yet we were still primarily inviting the lost to come to us. We were still in attractional mode.

Deep down, we didn't want to settle for people coming to faith. We wanted to build compassionate, generous, outward lives that reached across the divide and journeyed faith with unbelievers. We wanted a generous culture with mission at the heart of it; a culture where our lives naturally leaned toward the lost; a culture where people were intentional about leading people to God in every environment. We wanted *everyone, everywhere, everyday,* expressing their life in a way that led others into life.

That's what we wanted. But we didn't know how to go about it. We didn't know how to transition from hosting attractional services to unleashing missional movement.

All of that began to change the day I attended a Willow Creek conference in Cheltenham, England. It was everything Willow conferences ever are—inspiring, energizing, and galvanizing. It was hugely insightful and radically intentional about effectively creating churches that reach the lost and grow the found. Erwin McManus from Mosaic was the guest speaker at the conference. I had never heard Erwin before, but like everyone else, I was immediately engaged. His philosophy and journey toward outsiders resonated deeply with me.

During his message he stated that Mosaic had decided to make every ministry missional. It meant the entire church was on mission. Every environment was infused with a commitment to the outsider. If a ministry didn't connect with the unchurched community, the leaders of the church had a missional responsibility to close that ministry. As I listened, I knew God was speaking to me. We had just received a way to lead the entire church beyond the building.

Leading Found People Out to Life

Until then, we lacked a clear process for evaluating the effectiveness of our ministry environments. Now we had a clear, compelling way to assess alignment with our assignment. Now we measured the health of a ministry by its missional impact. If a ministry doesn't lead us toward lost people or lost people toward God, we don't do it. If it doesn't *include* the spiritually lost, *invest* in the lost, or impact the lost, we don't do it.

It doesn't matter if a ministry is growing or appears successful. If it's not missional, we don't do it.

It doesn't matter if it is marked by the supernatural. If it's not missional, we don't do it.

It doesn't matter if it's appealing or attractive. If it's not missional, we don't do it.

It doesn't matter if it's the next big thing in renewal. If it's not missional, we don't do it.

It doesn't matter if it serves huge pastoral needs. If it's not missional, we don't do it.

Every one of our ministries must connect with the unchurched community at some level.

This paradigm changed everything. From that moment, every aspect of our church life together gave equal value and priority to spiritually lost people. Leaders embraced their missional responsibility to close any ministry that failed to involve/invite/include outsiders within that first year.

Naturally, as a staff team, we wrestled hard with this tension. It provoked some of our most strenuous debates. It also became the birthing point for some of our most effective engagements with the community.

When we applied this to our kids' environments, we realized that to honor our commitment, we would have to close our Sunday school in a year unless we created a similar environment for children who were unreached and unchurched. As we considered this, our children's pastor, Dave, began to explore the idea of replicating our Sunday school in a local school.

We loved the idea but weren't entirely sure how to implement it. It's one thing to lead an assembly in a local school, but quite another to ask if you can host Sunday school there on a Friday afternoon. As it happened, our fears were groundless. Not only did the school agree to our request, but they also decided to condense and shorten the school day so the last hour of school could be devoted to our Sunday school. And so we began. Each week children stayed behind after class to engage with the kingdom. By the end of the year, we had more kids attend our Sunday school for the lost than our environment on Sunday morning for church kids.

After a few weeks, Dave invited some of the kids to say yes to God. And many of the kids with no prior church connection surrendered their young lives to Christ. We were shocked, but nothing could have prepared us for what happened next. Two weeks later, Dave invited the kids who had given their lives to Jesus to tell the others how God had changed their lives since they had become Christians.

One ten-year-old stood and told the class she had prayed for her grandmother who had been in hospital with cancer. Then she nonchalantly declared that her grandmother had been sent home and doesn't have the cancer anymore. After her story, a little boy stood to speak. He described how he, too, was learning to pray and had prayed to Jesus for his uncle who had kidney problems and was on a (dialysis) machine. Dave sat stunned as the boy said, "This week he doesn't need the machine anymore."

Both relatives were healed as kids who had known Christ for a matter of weeks prayed their best prayer. When Dave relayed the story to the rest of us at our weekly staff gathering, I sat there open-mouthed, thinking, *There it is again, the kingdom breaking out among the people.* It seemed like every time we disrupted our church community to show up in our wider community, the favor of the Father intensified.

These stories of outpouring kept us mission-critical when others were critical of our mission. They fueled our courage and propelled our commitment to move beyond evangelistic structures toward missional culture. Whenever we saw a small victory, we shared the story. When we shared the story, more people engaged and momentum increased.

Now we were learning to live lives around the value of generosity—giving away what God had given us. This included taking our church to the streets and to the poor, creating environments of encounter beyond the building. We began proactively sending missions teams. We appointed a missions pastor and began to explore just how far the kingdom would go "among the people." But it wasn't without loss and change and pain. We discovered that it's easier to *attend* a church that gathers lost people than *become* a people who change lost communities. We learned many valuable truths along the way:

- A church is measured by its sending capacity, not its seating capacity (as said by Rick Warren)
- We measured our *church health* by our *missional engagement*
- We aligned every ministry with our missional focus

- Equal priority meant equal time, energy, money, and focus
- If a ministry didn't lead us toward lost people or lost people toward Christ, we didn't do it
- We restructured our existing ministries around the value of compassionate generosity, with a fresh emphasis on reaching outsiders
- We developed new ministries and fresh environments outside the walls of the church, specifically designed with the lost in mind (including Healing on the Streets, Street Evangelism, Nightlight, and so on)
- We linked mission with spiritual formation and became a Sent Church

Our journey toward lost individuals and institutions was a much more difficult commitment than we ever anticipated *within* the church, and yet the Father continued to give us remarkable favor *outside* the church.

We harnessed outward focus in every area. Matthew 28:19 became as important in our thinking as Acts 15:19: "Therefore go and make disciples of all nations, baptizing them in the name of the Father and of the Son and of the Holy Spirit." We were becoming a community where every heart was invested. Finally, we were learning to go after the lost. We were learning to reposition the church to reach the city. We were learning to become scattered servants. Everyone, everywhere, everyday.

Reposition the Church to Reach the City

The pain of the transition was only eclipsed by the joy of a community that was learning to introduce the kingdom in their daily rhythms. This included our intern Rae, who dropped off a friend at the airport and stopped in at a department store on her way home. After picking up a couple of items, she went to the checkout. When she said good morning to the cashier, the girl commented on her accent. Rae told her she was from Brazil. Since we don't have too many folks from Brazil in Northern Ireland, the cashier was curious why Rae was in the area. So she told her, "I'm part of this team that goes into schools. I'm connected with the Vineyard church, and I'm here to tell people about Jesus. Do you know Jesus?" She replied that she didn't.

Rae began to tell her about Jesus and then asked, "Can I pray for you?" And the girl agreed. So Rae prayed for her, and as she prayed, the cashier began to weep and weep until eventually Rae asked, "Would you like to know Jesus?" The girl replied, "I'd love to." While a few people milled around the shop, Rae quietly prayed and the cashier opened her life to Jesus. Afterward, the cashier said, "I'm sorry. I'm not really in any fit state to process your order. Would you mind if I got one of my colleagues to come and do it instead?"

She called over a colleague who, upon arrival, asked the obvious question, "What happened?" Rae told her about the previous conversation, concluding with the question, "Do you know Jesus?" And the girl said, "No, I don't." Rae said, "Well, I'd love to tell you who He is." She began to describe Jesus to her. Then she asked, "Would it be okay if I prayed for you?" And the girl said yes.

As Rae began to pray, she had a picture of the cashier surrounded by all kinds of self-help books. She said, "I see that you're reading a lot in self-help and you suffer from depression, but what you need to know is that Jesus doesn't want you to waste your money on these books anymore. He is the Prince of Peace and He wants to come reveal Himself to you so you can save your money and get to know Him." At this, the girl started weeping and weeping. Rae said, "I can see you're really moved. Would you like to know Jesus?" And the girl said, "I really would." So Rae prayed for her, and she gave her life to Jesus too. Then the cashier said, "I'm not really in any fit state to process your order...."

At this point, Rae said she felt both excited and embarrassed because she started to wonder what people around her must be thinking she was saying to upset all these cashiers.

Undeterred, when the cashier called over a third colleague, and the third colleague asked, "What happened?" Rae just felt excited and blurted out, "You want to know what happened? Jesus happened. Do you know Jesus?" And the girl said, "No, I don't." So she began to tell her about Jesus and asked, "Can I pray for you?" The girl said, "I'd love for you to pray for me. I think I'm going to lose my job. I've got a terrible back condition. I've been off work so many days recently. I have a meeting with my manager this afternoon, and I think they're going to fire me. Could you pray for that?"

Rae prayed for her (this time secretly asking, "Oh, Jesus, please don't let her cry!"). She prayed for her to be healed and that

Jesus would reveal His heart to her. Afterward, the cashier tried moving her back. She was able to bend right over, and the pain was significantly improved. She gave her life to Jesus too. Thankfully this time, she was able to scan Rae's items, process the order, and Rae was finally able to leave the store.

It would never have happened in a gathered environment.

Chapter 6

EVERYONE EVERYDAY

The revered British evangelist Smith Wigglesworth once said, "It's not called the book of thoughts. It's called the book of Acts."[1]

It's called the book of Acts because the believers acted. They did something. The first believers didn't talk a lot about evangelism. It was in them, part of their DNA. A glance at Paul's missionary journeys shows he lived in a way that caused the kingdom to crash into the surrounding communities with remarkable power.

The early disciples moved with the message and lived with a mission. It wasn't something special but something normal. As they lived steeped in divine initiatives, these scattered servants brought life to every city they entered. It became inconceivable a community could remain the same when a servant showed up carrying the kingdom story.

And yet it didn't begin that way. As the book of Acts opens, there isn't very much ... action.

In Acts chapter 1, Jesus highlights the commission to become a movement of sent people witnessing to His words and works through the empowering of the Holy Spirit.[2] Acts chapter 2 begins with the promised *immersion* in the Holy Spirit and the first awakening of the Jewish community. It seems the early church didn't struggle reaching or attracting those who were lost. God added to their number daily those who were being saved.

And that was the problem.

What was intended to be a movement "of the found" quickly became a gathering "for the lost." And perhaps understandably so. Their gatherings were marked by exceptional power, demonstrable love, and tangible hope.

> They were continually devoting themselves to the apostles' teaching and to fellowship, to the breaking of bread and to prayer. Everyone kept feeling a sense of awe; and many wonders and signs were taking place through the apostles. And all those who had believed were together and had all things in common; and they began selling their property and possessions and were sharing them with all, as anyone might have need. Day by day continuing with one mind in the temple, and breaking bread from house to house, they were taking their meals together with gladness and sincerity of heart, praising God and having favor with all the people. And the Lord was adding to their number day by day those who were being saved.[3]

Who would want to leave an irresistible gathering like that?
Apparently no one.

As a community, they had spent three years traveling. It was
good to be all together in one place. Then the persecution arose,
and the dislocation, and all except the apostles were scattered
throughout Judea and Samaria.[4] Suddenly the church was mobile.
It wasn't intentional. But it was mobile. Those who were gathered
began to scatter. And those who had been scattered preached the
word *wherever* they went.[5]

Mission replaced location. Rumors circulated and reports began
to filter through of other places receiving favor:

> Philip went down to a city in Samaria and
> proclaimed the Messiah there. When the crowds
> heard Philip and saw the signs he performed, they
> all paid close attention to what he said. For with
> shrieks, impure spirits came out of many, and many
> who were paralyzed or lame were healed. So there
> was great joy in that city.[6]

Now cities were coming alive through the ministry of scattered
servants. And for a while it was the exception. Then it gathered
momentum.

> Those who had been scattered by the persecution
> that broke out when Stephen was killed traveled as
> far as Phoenicia, Cyprus and Antioch, spreading
> the word only among Jews. Some of them, however,

men from Cyprus and Cyrene, went to Antioch
and began to speak to Greeks also, telling them
the good news about the Lord Jesus. The Lord's
hand was with them, and a great number of people
believed and turned to the Lord.[7]

The power of the Lord was present with these servants. Wherever
they showed up, life followed. The Holy Spirit honored their words
and they demonstrated His works. Now more was happening
through scattered servants—empowered by the Spirit—than could
happen when the movement was confined to a particular location.

News of this reached the church in Jerusalem, and they sent
Barnabas to Antioch.[8]

When he arrived and saw what the grace of God had
done, he was glad and encouraged them all to remain
true to the Lord with all their hearts. He was a good
man, full of the Holy Spirit and faith, and a great
number of people were brought to the Lord.[9]

What Barnabas saw ignited his heart for more. It reminded him
of another person whose heart burned for everyone, everything,
everywhere to encounter the grace of God.

And so it was that Barnabas went to Tarsus to look for Saul.

Together Barnabas and Saul prayed and wondered and dreamed
of a movement of sent people. Together they longed for an expansive
expression of faith that went beyond the gathered environments.
Together they sensed that *they* would be part of such expansion, that

they had been set apart for such a movement. It wasn't long before the Holy Spirit confirmed their suspicions.

> While they were worshiping the Lord and fasting, the Holy Spirit said, "Set apart for me Barnabas and Saul for the work to which I have called them." So after they had fasted and prayed, they placed their hands on them and sent them off. The two of them, sent on their way by the Holy Spirit, went down to Seleucia and sailed from there to Cyprus.[10]

The Holy Spirit *sent* them on their way as scattered servants, *sent* them on their way to release the kingdom.

Scattered Servants Are Sent People

The word *sent* in Scripture is *apostolos*. It's not originally a biblical term. It's a cultural term. Jesus borrowed the language of culture to capture the imagination of His followers. Apostles were sent by the emperor/Caesar to establish the culture of the empire in various corners of the earth. Sent communities carry an expectation of introducing the culture of the kingdom and thereby infecting the culture of surrounding cities.

So as scattered servants they set about their Father's business of bringing life to cities. Scattered servants are sent people because God is a sending God. This has always been the case. When He heard the cries of broken people, He *sent* Moses into Egypt.[11] When humanity drifted from design, He *sent* His prophets to the people to remind them of glorious favor and warn them of the consequences of rebellion. He *sent* John the Baptist to prepare the way for the Lord. He so loved the world that He *sent* His only Son.[12]

Jesus then *sent* the early followers as scattered servants to the uttermost parts of the earth. "As the Father has sent me, I am sending you."[13]

When Jesus spoke the words "so send I you," He was commissioning them (and by extension us) to operate with the same authority and assignment as He had. His assignment was not a mystery. His assignment was to bring life. We know this because He told us. "I have come so that you might have life."[14] But life doesn't come until someone is sent.

This is why, throughout the Scriptures, people are sent. We are sent the same way as Jesus Himself was sent—in glory, authority, humility, and vulnerability.

The church is the group of people … *sent to bring life … to cities and regions and nations.*

God doesn't send the lost into the church. He sends the found into the world. And now in response to the brokenness all around, He sends us!

Almighty God has made a promise to the city and the broken. It's called the church. The church is not only the gathered environment—it is the sent, the scattered servants. Everyone. Everywhere. Everyday. As a result, the church at its best is not sitting asking God to unleash hope *to* hurting hearts. The church is at its best when it knows it has been sent by God to unleash hope *in* hurting hearts.

God always answers the cries and longings of hurting humanity with the words "so send I you."

The Shift from Commitment to Compassion

Our calling and mission is to carry the kingdom beyond the church into the heart of culture. As sent people, the core of the church is no longer defined as those who support the structure *of* church, but those who are transforming culture *as* church. The "core" are not those who give and serve to keep the church going or growing; the core are those who risk to release the kingdom. Their primary loyalty is no longer to church activity.

Nonetheless, releasing scattered servants does not involve abandonment of gathered environments. Gathering together is of central importance throughout Scripture. What God can do in individuals is exceptional. What He does in community is exponential. There is great favor in gathering together; but (as the church at Antioch discovered when they sent Paul and Barnabas) there is greater favor beyond our gatherings.

Our quest to develop excellence in our gathered environments has produced a reticence in releasing scattered servants. It is just hard to release people to run with their God-given vision when we need them to run with ours. We cannot allow those sent by God to be stifled by the church. We must let them run with what God has spoken uniquely to them. And we must let them rule over what God has entrusted to them.

"Let them rule" is the divine permission inscribed at creation. The *permission* is always for *mission*. And the mission is always to bring life to every corner of culture.

According to Scripture, every believer is a trusted ruler, called by God to lead the earth into life. This is the original mandate that has never been rescinded.[15] Trusted rulers know their identity, understand their spiritual authority, and introduce life to the city. While volunteers may meet the needs of the church, only the emergence of trusted rulers can fuel the dreams of the city.

It's time to stop raising up volunteers at the expense of trusted rulers. It's time to stop trying to get people to "buy into the vision" of the church and begin releasing people to run with the vision God has given them—releasing them to be sources of hope addressing the needs of the city and unlocking the dreams of the city.

Controlling and Directing versus Creativity and Honor

I admire the courage of the church in Antioch. It's challenging to send good people. It's especially difficult sending them to do something different from what you have ever done. Allowing people to run and rule requires a different leadership posture. It shifts us from controlling and directing to creativity and honor. Letting people run involves relinquishing control. This means leaders releasing people to create compassion centers and ministry centers in the community. It means learning to say yes to ministry and releasing control. At Causeway Coast Vineyard, every idea gets a yes, but not all get resourced. We want our policies to unleash possibilities. It has led to increased life, increased mess, increased energy, increased failure, increased hearts, increased influence, and increased fatigue.

Truthfully, it's easier to lead from control than creativity. It's just not what we're called to do.

Letting people rule involves releasing them to operate with spiritual authority and sacrificial love in a way that leads their area of involvement into alignment with the Father. As we make this shift, kingdom people lead the city into life in thousands of unimaginable creative ways, causing transformation in every environment through presence, wisdom, and kingdom solutions.

Dee Hock, the founder and former CEO of the Visa credit card company, coined the term "chaordic organization," which means blending the qualities of *chaos* and *order*. When this amalgamation occurs, she says, the organization becomes "a living set of beliefs."[16] This should be the goal of sending churches—achieving the vibrancy of blending chaos and order, as we release people to fully follow their vision and utilize their gifts beyond the church building. We create generous space where people can come alive and lead others into life. It means that the core of our church is happening out there in the community.

Church Planting versus People Planting

Twenty years ago, we thought planting churches was the key to changing cities. Citadels of hope are always necessary. We still need more churches, better churches. But we need something more: messengers of hope, believers who carry the culture of the kingdom into the ordinary moments of life.

For a long time, Richard had nurtured the idea for opening a gym. His last business venture hadn't been entirely successful, so it took significant faith to dream again. But his heart was stirred by the desire to create a space where strength and conditioning occurred in a family-friendly atmosphere. While still in the dreaming stage, Richard was encouraged by several prophetic voices. He persevered against a background of limited funds, knowing God was able to do more than he thought possible. Eventually high-quality facilities were obtained and the doors opened.

Today the gym is flourishing. Richard is considering expansion into other areas and is investing in other dreams and dreamers. In fact, facilitating the dreams of others is a vital part of the company culture. Richard says, "We will help to unleash the passion of our employees (and staff connected to our organization), thus allowing them to become agents of change spreading our culture of care throughout our community." But the dream is for more than their company. The dream is for a better city, and so 5 percent of their profit is invested and donated to "support the effectiveness of the nonprofit sector and improve the community where we live and work." It's a core dream. It's a kingdom dream. It's what happens when the Spirit of God rests upon scattered servants.

The shift from church planting to people planting redefines what it looks like to lead our cities into life. Usually we plant churches by carefully recruiting people to our vision, often missing the opportunity to release them in their solution. It's tempting (even prevalent) to centralize solutions and operate with a program mind-set. When we send scattered servants, we treat them as trusted rulers and invite them to listen to Jesus, be guided by the Spirit, steward a solution from heaven, and release it into the earth.

This is the way it was always meant to be.

The Wind Blows Wherever It Wants

We read in John 3:8 (NIV), "The wind blows wherever it pleases. You hear its sound, but you cannot tell where it comes from or where it is going. So it is with everyone born of the Spirit."

It's a haunting verse. It reminds me that those immersed in the presence live uncontainable, uncontrollable lives. It reminds me as a church leader that my authority exists to supply destiny. It reminds me that it is not my church. It reminds me that these are not my people. It reminds me that their primary loyalty is not to church activity. These are not merely *supportive* servants, assigned by God to strengthen my vision or assist with church expansion. Under the influence of the Spirit, they show up wherever they please, bringing life to everyone they meet.

The wind blows wherever it pleases—and so it is with *everyone* born of the Spirit.

This awakens me to the possibility that everyone can be part of the divine movement. It reminds me that God is doing way more through the movement of His people than I can imagine. It encourages me that the kingdom advances through servants, not experts. It reassures me that the kingdom is so much more expansive than our services. As a leader, it invites me to unleash the power of everyone, everywhere, everyday.

One evening around Christmastime, a small group in our church decided they would go for a walk in the local community during their weekly meeting instead of having a teaching time. As they were walking, a group member named Phil heard some wind chimes and sensed Jesus telling him, "Go to the house where the wind chimes are." So he listened again for the sound and began moving in their direction. Eventually he found the house and knocked on the door. Upstairs someone shuffled, peered through the curtains, then came down the stairs. Since there were six locks on the door, it took a while for it to open. It was clear that whoever lived there was living in fear.

When the door opened, Phil smiled and asked, "Is there anything we can pray for you tonight?" The guy who opened the door started into his story. His brother had died in the previous few weeks. Another close relative had died six months earlier, compounding this man's pain. The man was alone and afraid. Although he wasn't a Christian, the abyss of his pain moved him to pray. So that night he cried out to God to send someone to help him. And now here was Phil standing at his door offering to pray. Here was a scattered servant sent with Spirit authority to introduce someone to his divine destiny.

On another occasion, Phil and the team were helping with the lesson in a local school. As they unpacked Scripture with the students, one kid declared, "I don't believe it." Phil probed a little, asking, "What would it take for you to believe that the stuff written in this book was true?" The girl replied, "I'll believe it when I see it." Ordinarily that argument would suffice and end the discussion. But the girl didn't know that Phil was a kingdom carrier and excited at the prospect of demonstrating the kingdom.

Phil called out to the kids in the room, "Is there anyone here with pain in his or her body?" Silence. He continued, "There is someone here experiencing pain in your back, and God wants to heal you right now."

Reluctantly, one of the students responded. Phil explained that this is often caused by misalignment of the spine and often rectified through growing the leg. Turning to the girl who had expressed her skepticism, Phil said, "Do you want to see a leg grow?" And then he commanded the leg to grow. And the leg grew.

Having introduced the kingdom, Phil invited the kids to encounter the King. Six of them did, including the girl who now believed because she had seen.

It never crossed Phil's mind that the story could have ended differently. It certainly crossed mine. Aside from potentially disappointing the kids, the incident could have disrupted our relationship with the school. The safe option is to leave *that* stuff until *after* class. The safe option is only to do things with permission.

Had Phil asked for my wisdom, I would have counseled him to handle things differently. Thankfully he didn't ask. Scattered servants need to be entrusted and empowered by leaders to take their own risks and to make their own mistakes.

It's impossible to raise up safe scattered servants. They are systemically unsafe! As leaders, we try to control release in our gathered environments and release control of scattered servants. It's difficult for people to know God trusts them if we don't trust them. Scattered servants need to be entrusted if they are to be empowered.

The wind is blowing wherever it pleases and moving everything in its path, shifting atmospheres, changing cities. The next great move of God is already occurring—even now it is upon us. It's easy to miss it because it is not centralized—it is mobilized. It is happening beyond the building. It's happening in our everyday, ordinary lives.

Chapter 7

EVERYWHERE EVERYDAY

David had been a Christian for years, attended church regularly, and was active in his faith. Yet he had never awakened to the kingdom at work in his everyday life. Not long after he first attended Causeway Coast Vineyard, we started a short three-week series entitled "Wake Up, Sleeper." We began each talk with a drum solo while we collectively read Ephesians 5:15. Something stirred in David. Each morning he entered his workplace, headed for his office, and the sound from the Sunday would begin coursing through his head. God was activating his faith and his authority at work.

I'll let him tell the unfolding story:

> Recently I prayed for the father of one our staff
> members and have seen his life change overnight as

a result. Chains of addiction have been completely broken!

Another member of our staff has joined our men's group after several conversations at work about small groups. He was looking for something on the very night we had the group.

At the same time, I have been praying for another staff family member who had been diagnosed with a terminal disease and given two months to live. Seven months on, those prayers continue to be answered. I've also seen impossible deadlines met. In one case after prayer, I went into a high-level meeting with a government stakeholder in the face of a desperate situation. I was ready to ask for their help, but instead was asked for my help by them, with all my needs met in full!

Since our agreement in church to "live out more," I've seen knees healed, cancer sufferers being given the all-clear, and had the privilege of leading another member of staff to faith, someone my colleague and I have been praying with.

With that in mind, as someone in senior management, I met with the guys from the Causeway Coast Vineyard Compassion Team to see how we could partner. Since that meeting last year, we were able to have some of the Foodbank staff at a student event, and Vineyard Compassion members stand at our Health and Wellbeing event for staff.

As a result, a Christians Against Poverty course is being arranged for one of our classes of students, and there are plans for Foodbank Collection Points across all of our campuses, with the ability to refer students.

I've just this week been working on ideas for our next Health and Wellbeing staff event, and we hope to have Foodbank and Clothing Bank collections as part of the day. Things are moving slowly but they are moving.

Scattered servants release the kingdom everywhere, everyday. It's what we were made for. We were made to step into the story, breaking out beyond our services, study groups, and strategy meetings. We were made for a story bigger than church, greater than culture.

Your Everyday, Ordinary Life

"So here's what I want you to do, God helping you: Take your everyday, ordinary life—your sleeping, eating, going-to-work, and walking-around life—and place it before God as an offering."[1]

Take your everyday, ordinary life and live it generously, radically, expansively, creatively, courageously, compassionately, redemptively. Live it gloriously. Live in His story. Live out your story. Live knowing that God is with you, He's for you, and He is in you.

God ordains your ordinary. Yet there remains a tendency to separate the miraculous from menial. When that happens, our life at work becomes divorced from our faith. This is dangerous because when we fail to see the story of God at work, we miss the opportunity to partner with God at work and other commonplace contexts. And so we begin dividing work into sacred and secular: jobs that release the kingdom and jobs that resist the kingdom; the important and irrelevant; regular employment and kingdom assignment.

So God invites us to rethink everything we are and everything we do, through the lens of mercy. "I urge you, brothers and sisters, in view of God's mercy, to offer your bodies as a living sacrifice, holy and pleasing to God—this is your true and proper worship."[2] The vision of expansive grace infiltrates our everyday story. Gripped by mercy, we slowly understand that God's mercy is everywhere, for everyone. Gradually, instead of *colliding*, our faith and work *connect*. Instead of wrestling with the dilemma of quitting our jobs to pursue kingdom ministry, we realize that our job is kingdom ministry.

Ordinary Ministry, Everyday Glory

A couple of years ago, large numbers of people in our community came to faith. Many came as a result of catalytic evangelists who spent their time on the streets helping people say yes to God. Initially everyone applauded and soon they wanted to be involved too.

What ensued was a wonderful reorientating of lives "beyond ourselves," but the subtle shift that accompanied this was not healthy or helpful at all. People began to believe that the real work of the kingdom was *only* happening in the streets. It wasn't long before some began questioning the relevance and significance of their lives at work. It felt mundane rather than meaningful. After all, "nobody ever tells stories from stages of spreadsheets ... of cleaning ... of work done well."[3]

Scattered servants are not *stolen* from the workplace. They are sent to the workplace. The kingdom is not an escape from real work; it is an engagement with real work. Kingdom carriers are jewelers and gardeners, carpenters and bricklayers, shopkeepers and engineers, lawyers and doctors, architects and designers.

If we are to fulfill our mandate of bringing life to everything everywhere, we must see our involvement in institutions and industries and workplaces as kingdom work. We must reject the idea that kingdom work happens mainly in services, on stages, or on street corners and respond to God's invitation to join Him in His work of reshaping the world in ordinary places like shopping centers, farms, factories, and offices.

Bring Back Life to the Workplace

When I first became a believer, I connected with a local church in a deprived housing estate. It was a new church, largely composed of young adults recently set free from addiction. Although the church was marked by passionate spirituality, it viewed those engaged in employment rather suspiciously. Work seemed like a distraction from destiny rather than a doorway into it. We had changed the divine story to fit our reality rather than changing our reality to fit the story.

The story is that work originated in the heart of God. It was His idea, His initiative. Here's how it began:

> The LORD God formed a man from the dust of the
> ground and breathed into his nostrils the breath
> of life, and the man became a living being. Now
> the LORD God had planted a garden in the east, in
> Eden; and there he put the man he had formed....
> The LORD God took the man and put him in the
> Garden of Eden to work it and take care of it.[4]

As the story opens, God breathes life into humanity (literally inspires them) and then instructs them to bring life to their environment.[5] We don't just go to work. We are sent to work. Work is where humanity learns to breathe out what God has breathed into us. We learn in the work environment what it means to become fully human, to flourish, to connect with the story of God.

Our work was intended to be a place of discovery and creativity, not only productivity. As someone once said, we don't just work to earn; we work to learn. Fundamentally, we work to create, explore, and innovate. And as Adam cultivated and shaped the garden around him, God shaped something within Adam. But He also shaped something with him. Like Adam, you are working for God—more than that, you are working *with* God. He invites us to take our place beside Him, to work with Him for the transformation of the workplace.

It's time to integrate what has been separated: Your vocation and your vision. Your spiritual journey and your job. Your job and your joy. Your industry and your ministry. Your connection with God and your connection with the world.

Regardless of where you work and what you do, your job is your kingdom assignment. You are not employed, you are assigned. An assignment is a specific calling to effect change in an environment. Therefore, as kingdom believers, we are not called to survive the workplace, but to seek its transformation. You can accomplish this by recognizing that God's Spirit is upon you at work, just as everywhere else.

Indeed, the workplace was the first place where humanity was filled with the Spirit:

> Then the LORD said to Moses, "See, I have chosen Bezalel son of Uri, the son of Hur, of the tribe of Judah, and I have filled him with the Spirit of God, with wisdom, with understanding, with knowledge and with all kinds of skills—to make artistic designs for work in gold, silver and bronze, to cut and set stones, to work in wood, and to engage in all kinds of crafts."[6]

Bezalel was a craftsman inspired by the Spirit of God, called to inscribe the story of God through his work. His skills at work were tangible evidence of the Spirit at work. God anointed Bezalel *at* his work and God anointed Bezalel *as* he worked. Therefore, Bezalel's workplace was a place of divine presence. And in that workplace, God moved upon Bezalel, revealing Himself to others through this craftsman's work. His vocation was filled with the vision of God.

Sadly our workplace is sometimes considered a place of divine absence. It's the place where we show up without expecting God to show up. Yet scattered servants understand that every workplace is a place of His presence. It's not only possible to encounter God at work, it's normal. God is at work in our work. Our work matters to God, and anything that matters to God carries His favor. We can experience His presence in us, with us, and on us as we work.

One day, my brother, John, was getting ready for work when he sensed the Holy Spirit speak to him about one of his colleagues. God showed him that her mother had recently been hospitalized due to arthritis. Upon arrival at work, John asked to speak privately with his colleague and explained what God had shown him earlier that morning. She confirmed what he said was accurate and was responsive to prayer.

Afterward, she was so impacted that she told her workmates, who eagerly asked John if God had spoken anything to him for them. He informed them that as yet he had heard nothing, but would pray and share whatever he heard with them the next day. Anticipation filled the air as John returned to work the next day. Although none of his colleagues were believers, all of them were open to spiritual things. As John shared what he believed God had shown him, a stunned silence filled the office as his work colleagues realized ... God knew them.

An office space became a holy place.

This happened for the entire week; each day John declared in public what the Father had shown him privately. At the end of the week, Father God spoke to John about the colleague with whom he had developed the closest relationship. He told him that the man and his partner were eager to have kids but had fertility problems. John wisely didn't want to share this in the office, so he invited his friend for lunch. Over lunch he shared his insight, and as he did, the man began to cry. Even though John had worked closely with him for years, he had no idea he was infertile. Yet God knew.

The Supernatural and the Supra-narrative

As we partner with God at work, we minister His presence to others. We learn to lean into divine whispers and promptings. We listen to what God might speak to individuals. We pray for cancer and arthritis to be overthrown. We counsel our coworkers, we share our hope, we lead others to faith. All of these are the work of the Spirit at work in our work. But the same Spirit who rests upon us for the sake of individuals also rests upon us for the sake of entire industries.[7]

We want more than occasional ministry; we want to see "kingdom industries"—whole workplaces that release good; jobs created that provide dignity, industries immersed in divine reality, individuals aware that their work makes the kingdom available and transforms culture.

Every life-giving industry was designed by God and destined for God. His voice and vision are over it all. Scripture reminds us, "The earth is the LORD's, and everything in it."[8] And, "The whole earth will be filled with the glory of the knowledge of God."[9] Therefore, God has infused every workplace with glory. God has written promises over industries. His blessing rests upon trades as diverse as engineering, education, and entertainment.

Scattered servants are harnessed to the supernatural and the supra-narrative. Their story is God's story. They understand how being a house cleaner connects with the kingdom, how being a businessman reaches much further than profitability, how being a schoolteacher supplies destiny, how being a pastor invites partnership with the city so that everyone, everywhere can come alive to the mercy, the story, and the glory of God. Then they creatively partner with God to release the optimal potential of the working environment and the industry where they work.

What if we entered the story of God concerning architecture, engineering, bio-sciences, and technologies?

What if we asked about the original design for industries?

What if we moved from simply inviting God into our workspace to innovating with God?

What if we captured the kingdom assignment in our employment?

What if God was inviting you to work together with Him to bring back life to your industry?

What if we moved from resenting work to being sent to work?

Ordination of the Ordinary

At the end of my Bible college studies, there was a commissioning service designed to remind us that God had uniquely gifted and called each one to serve. It was beautiful and memorable. And yet it strikes me how the vast majority of us rarely enjoy such a moment of ordination/commissioning for our regular jobs. We resent our work because we have never been sent to work in the local company by the local church.

We don't associate commissioning and prayers of blessing with jobs outside the ministry of the church. But in the Bible this was normal practice. When Isaac blessed Jacob, he blessed his business: your flocks will grow, your inheritance will increase, your business will excel, you'll become known as a good businessman in the community. The pattern continued in the next generation with Jacob and his sons. There was always blessing, not only on individuals and their families, but on their businesses and enterprises. It would have been inconceivable to conduct business without blessing.

Jesus commissioned His disciples to bring life to every place and every space, to unleash and unlock the kingdom. It was the same pattern of blessing intended to transform the whole of society. I paraphrase Matthew 28:19–20: "Therefore go (to your workplace) and make disciples (be a teacher) of all nations (your coworkers), baptizing (immersing) them in the name (the nature and identity) of the Father and of the Son and of the Holy Spirit, and teaching them (by your example) to obey everything I have commanded you. And surely I am with you always, to the very end of the age."

It's time to see everything, everywhere filled with ordinary glory. It's time to ordain hairdressers and Uber drivers, engineers and baristas as kingdom carriers. It's time to release filmmakers and poets, lawyers and doctors. It's time to anoint people to teach in church and teach in schools. It's time to recognize apostles and architects. It's time to bless the missionary and the machinist. It's time to pray for the young woman heading to seminary to study theology and for the young man heading to university to study fashion.

It's time to ordain the ordinary. We do so knowing that the next great move of God is not going to be a movement *in* the church. It's going to be a movement *of* the church *into* society, rewriting the story of education in our cities, health in our cities, and business in our cities. God is repositioning the church to reach the whole city, with believers communicating, demonstrating, and celebrating the supremacy of Christ in every corner of culture.

Chapter 8

ENCOUNTERING THE SUPERNATURAL BEYOND THE BUILDING

The supernatural is not peripheral to our lifestyle. It is central. The gospel movement is a movement ... with power. There is no power without the gospel,[1] but there is no gospel without power.[2]

Often the power of God shows up before the people of God.

Andrew attended one of our courses on dream interpretation.[3] He listened as we explored the various occasions in ancient Scripture—and in our experience—where God used dreams to draw people into life-giving relationship. When the course finished, he returned to his hometown to visit his mother-in-law, who had recently been admitted to hospital. When he arrived, he noticed an old man without any visitors. Andrew decided to help alleviate the man's loneliness. He discovered the man was eighty-nine years old and his wife had died the previous year. Then he asked a question we all ask those in a hospital. "Are you sleeping all right?" The man smiled wistfully as he told Andrew that he slept wonderfully and that every night he had the same dream.

The man explained that each night he dreams he is back in the war. He is standing in a field, and at the bottom of the field is a house. He walks toward the house and upon entering discovers that those inside have been expecting him. The man said they use the same phrase every time. As they show him to the dining table, they say, "We have prepared a place for you," and as they show him to his room, they say, "We have prepared a place for you." Then the dream ends.

Andrew knew this was a divine appointment. He looked at the man and said, "Would you like to know what your dream means?" The man nodded enthusiastically as Andrew opened the Scriptures to John 14:1–3:

> Do not let your hearts be troubled. You believe in God; believe also in me. My Father's house has many rooms; if that were not so, would I have told you that I am going there to prepare a place for you? And if I go and prepare a place for you, I will come back and take you to be with me that you also may be where I am.

Andrew asked the man if he believed in God. The man answered, "I have always believed God exists." Andrew continued, "This verse also says you have to believe in Jesus and trust Him with your life.

Have you ever trusted Him with your life?" The man paused, then shook his head. "Would you like to do that now?" So the eighty-nine-year-old man surrendered his life to the God who had been speaking to him every night for months.

Often the power of God shows up *before* the people of God. Sometimes the power of God shows up *with* the people of God.

Scott led Donna to faith a few weeks before he met with her partner, Robert. Robert requested the meeting because he was concerned Donna's newfound faith was stirring tension in their relationship. He wanted to meet to straighten things out. Scott wanted to meet so he could lead Robert to life. The initial exchanges were terse. Gradually Robert warmed to Scott's personality but remained unconvinced by his message. Scott again shared his story and the story of Jesus. Still nothing. "Would you mind if we prayed?" Scott asked. Robert agreed, so Scott prayed and as he did he broke some demonic influences operating around Robert.

Afterward, he looked up, and although Robert was moved, he wasn't ready to begin a relationship with Jesus. Robert explained, "I just don't want to take the risk of giving up drugs for something that isn't real." Scott began to pray, "Lord, show me the key to this man's heart." A thought flashed through his mind as he prayed, and before he had time to think on it, words poured from his lips. "I am going to pray for you right now and a wind is going to enter this coffee shop, swirl around your head, and you will know in that moment that God is real, He loves you, and is pursuing a relationship with you." So Scott prayed, the wind came, and Robert surrendered his life to the One who had pursued him all his days.

Occasionally the power of God shows up *after* the people of God.

The team we had trained to do healing on the streets in Edinburgh was praying for a man who had broken his knee. As they prayed their best prayer, they asked him to try it out to see if there was any change. There wasn't. The man left and continued his journey down the street. When he turned the corner onto the next street, the power of God fell on this unsuspecting unbeliever and he tumbled to the ground. Those who witnessed him fall thought he was seriously ill and immediately called for an ambulance. The paramedics examined him and gave him the all-clear. So he stood up, and as he did, he realized his broken knee was healed.

Sent to Demonstrate the Kingdom with Power

We want more than powerful moments *in* church; we want power *as* church.

The Spirit of God was not given for exciting church services but to empower scattered servants. He wasn't given so we could have better meetings or greater experiences. He was sent so we could be sent ... with power. And so we could bear witness to a powerful Christer.[4] "You will receive power when the Holy Spirit comes on you; and you will be my witnesses."[5] While the power of the Holy Spirit was given *to us*, it wasn't given *for us*. Kingdom power was given to bring wholeness to the whole of humanity.

His Spirit rests on us to reach our cities. In the process, He renews our churches. But the purpose is to release whole cities.

His Spirit comes upon us for the sake of our cities, not so we can develop our ministries. Yet for too long we have believed the lie that empowered ministry is principally concerned with making space for the supernatural in our services. We have settled for phenomenal services instead of power on our streets. We have settled for experiencing renewal instead of bringing life. While renewal is to be desired, it is too low a goal. Kingdom power isn't for bringing life to otherwise dull services; it belongs to servants.

And scattered servants refuse to confine the kingdom to a church service or church people. It took us a long time to learn that the power was given for the lost, not for the church.

Healing on the Streets

I still remember the first time we ventured out to pray for healing on the streets of our town.[6] I wish I could say I was full of faith. More accurately, I was full of fear. I was stewarding the open secret. The open secret—in most churches—is that we have a theology of healing and we pray for healing, yet most people we pray for don't get healed. Moreover, we are somewhat surprised if they do get healed.

As a Vineyard pastor, this was a little embarrassing to me. I felt fraudulent.

I desperately longed for broken lives and bodies to be healed; I just didn't see it very much. Over the years, I had grown tired of reciting the reasons why so many people didn't get healed. I wanted to witness the invasion of God's goodness. I guess that was part of the attraction of John Wimber's ministry for me. When he prayed at conferences, people seemed to get healed. And now here was I, a Vineyard pastor, carrying around the open secret that no one was really getting healed.

So when my friend Mark Marx invited me to pray for people on the streets, I felt a little like one of David's men, who said to him, "Here in Judah we are afraid. How much more, then, if we go to Keilah against the Philistine forces!"[7] Similarly, I thought, *This stuff doesn't work in-house. What on earth makes you think it would work outside the church?* It seemed back to front. Surely we should get good at healing Christians, go out full of stories, brimming with victories, and then open the kingdom to the lost. Since we had not experienced much healing presence in the church, I assumed divine absence in the community.

I could not have been more wrong.

The first person to take a seat was an Indian lady. She was suffering from arthritis in her knees. Mark explained how some conditions are caused or influenced by misalignment of the body and asked if the woman had one leg shorter than the other. Sure enough, her one leg was shorter than the other. Not just a little shorter. Really short. So short, I am amazed she didn't spend her days walking in circles.

While I was processing her leg length and wondering what we were going to do, Mark was already boldly inviting people to witness a miracle. As he prayed—more accurately, commanded—her leg grew immediately. Then she told us the arthritis in her knee had been instantly healed.

I was stunned. I had no framework for fruitfulness.

By the time I recovered my senses, the lady was already on her way fifty yards down the street. So I did what all good pastors do … I chased her. When I finally caught up with her, I blurted out, "I am the pastor of the church that guy attends. It's okay if you didn't get healed. You can tell me." She looked at me quizzically, confirmed her healing, and continued on her journey, looking taller with every step.

She never looked back, and I couldn't go back. We had encountered the supernatural on a Saturday afternoon, and I didn't want to ever confine it to Sunday mornings again.

The Church Has Largely Lost Sight of God's Power

The church at large has limited God's ability. Believers enter most environments without expectation of intervention. We have embraced a theology more akin to determinism than deliverance. We have been crushed by disappointment rather than overwhelmed by wonder. In general, the expectation of God's supernatural power has been abandoned. If not abandoned, it has been reserved for gathered environments rather than the normal experience of scattered servants who use their authority to rewrite the story of the city.

The great need of our day is scattered servants, kingdom carriers who have learned to move beyond phenomena in services to release power in their everyday lives.

Edna had only been given a few months to live. Like many people who show up on our streets to be prayed for, she had been brought by a concerned family member. As the team talked with her, they discovered she had a rare form of cancer affecting her bladder and liver, and that she was scheduled to have an operation in the coming days. The team, as they always do, prayed their best prayer, but it wasn't until a few weeks later that they heard what happened next.

Edna was admitted to hospital for her operation as planned. The operation was scheduled to last eight hours and involved five teams of surgeons. After anesthetizing Edna, the surgeons made the necessary incisions in her body only to discover the cancer had completely disappeared.

Edna's story is wonderful yet increasingly common. It is no longer surprising to encounter the supernatural beyond the building. Indeed, in the last few years, we have received numerous reports of cancer being healed. What is remarkable, though, is not *that* people are being healed or indeed that cancers are being healed, but *where* people are being healed. They are being healed on our streets.

And not just on our streets, but on streets all over what is considered secular Europe.

The Word of the Lord Spread and Grew in Power

We have the privilege of hearing firsthand how street corners are becoming ministry centers and how the church is moving from renewal to releasing the power of the kingdom. Stories like the following from a Healing on the Streets team in Birmingham, England, provide an example:

> We recently had a Hindu lady who came back to us to let us know that she had been healed. She had been prayed for twelve months ago for boils she had all over her body. She said she had

been to see many doctors and specialists and was on steroids. She also said that she had spent over £4000 on different treatments. She returned to tell us that she was prayed for at *hots* and woke up the next morning to find the boils had completely gone. She returned with a photo to remind us what she looked like twelve months ago, which showed three big boils on her face. She held it up to her face, which now has completely smooth and unblemished skin!

And then there's this account from a Healing on the Streets team in Oslo, Norway:

Incredible, increasing, awesome amazing day at Egertorget last Saturday.... Many healed of back pain, neck problems, knee problems, and foot issues. The team prayed for more than forty people. A total of twenty-six physical conditions were healed while many others were touched by God's love. One person told us that we prayed for him to be healed of diabetes type 1 in October. A few days later, he went to his doctor and took a blood test. The blood test was normal. After the fifth time of testing his blood daily, they took him off the medicine because he didn't have diabetes anymore! A real breakthrough and good fun.

And one final story from a Healing on the Streets team in Kenya:

> We were doing door-to-door evangelism one afternoon (essentially this was walking miles and miles from one homestead to another in the middle of the bush in Massai heartland). We would show up on a farm, the whole family would gather outside their mud huts, and we shared Jesus with them all. Once each team shared the gospel, we prayed for the sick. God moved powerfully and healed those with illness. Then usually all who hadn't previously committed their lives to Christ would surrender their hearts to Him.
>
> On one occasion, a family of eleven gathered and heard the gospel. The youngest member of the family was a five-year-old boy who was completely deaf. We prayed for him, and he instantly received his hearing. The family tested his healing by sending him outside the house and calling to him. And he responded every time they called. He returned to the home and then all eleven family members decided to surrender their hearts to Jesus.
>
> By the end of our week, we were ready to plant a church in this area. And so on Sunday, 13 February, in the middle of a field in a marquee (with not a building in sight), we planted a church. Many who had encountered Jesus throughout the week came that day. The meeting ended up being some

> hundred- to a hundred-and-fifty strong, and even
> as we left we realized that many were still emerging
> from the bush, having spent all day walking miles to
> reach the "church" (marquee). It was overwhelming
> to see God's kingdom breaking out—for healings,
> signs and wonders, and the best of all *salvations!*

We could fill several books with stories of remarkable healings, signs, and wonders occurring through ordinary believers in extraordinary places. All of them are scattered servants releasing the supernatural beyond the building. The sick are being healed in hospitals, parks, racecourses, public squares, swimming pools, schools, factories, airports ... everywhere!

While these stories are wonderful, they pale in comparison to what happened in Ephesus. That city was a cultural epicenter that seemed impregnable to the gospel. But when scattered servants showed up in Ephesus, the entire city became vulnerable to the nearness and goodness of God.

> This went on for two years, so that all the Jews and
> Greeks who lived in the province of Asia heard the
> word of the Lord. God did extraordinary miracles
> through Paul, so that even handkerchiefs and
> aprons that had touched him were taken to the sick,
> and their illnesses were cured and the evil spirits
> left them.... Many of those who believed now
> came and openly confessed what they had done. A
> number who had practiced sorcery brought their

scrolls together and burned them publicly. When they calculated the value of the scrolls, the total came to fifty thousand drachmas. In this way the word of the Lord spread widely and grew in power.[8]

The whole city was turned upside down through a community intentionally demonstrating the kingdom with compassion and authority. Although these events are unusual in recent times, they were intended to be indicative of what is available in every generation.[9]

The Kingdom Is Constantly Pervasive and Gradually Prevailing

We know this because Jesus told us that is what the kingdom of God is like: "The kingdom of heaven is like a mustard seed, which a man took and planted in his field. Though it is the smallest of all seeds, yet when it grows, it is the largest of garden plants and becomes a tree, so that the birds come and perch in its branches."[10]

The illustration of a mustard seed was frequently used by Jesus to nudge people toward kingdom insight. In one instance, He employs it to explain the kingdom crashing into a woman who needed freedom.

On a Sabbath Jesus was teaching in one of the synagogues, and a woman was there who had been crippled by a spirit for eighteen years. She was bent over and could not straighten up at all. When Jesus saw her, he called her forward and said to her,

"Woman, you are set free from your infirmity." Then he put his hands on her, and immediately she straightened up and praised God.

Indignant because Jesus had healed on the Sabbath, the synagogue leader said to the people, "There are six days for work. So come and be healed on those days, not on the Sabbath."

The Lord answered him, "You hypocrites! Doesn't each of you on the Sabbath untie your ox or donkey from the stall and lead it out to give it water? Then should not this woman, a daughter of Abraham, whom Satan has kept bound for eighteen long years, be set free on the Sabbath day from what bound her?"

When he said this, all his opponents were humiliated, but the people were delighted with all the wonderful things he was doing.[11]

It seemed the religion scholars were questioning why God breaks rules to reach people.

Which brings us back to mustard seeds.

Mustard seeds were an unlikely choice for a holy parable. Of all seeds, the mustard seed is most messy and most likely to result in uncleanness.[12] By planting the seed in a garden, the gardener risked breaking the law.[13] The point of the parable is not that the mustard seed is the biggest, but that it gets *everywhere*. It expands. It expands beyond our ability to contain or control. And once loose, it takes over. It becomes a gathering point for outsiders. We can't keep it confined or contained. This is what the kingdom is like. When the kingdom is alive in us, it alters the environments around us. And so Jesus risked healing one woman and it unleashes something in the community—the repercussions of that event are enormous. It leads to everyone knowing that God will break the rules to reach the people.

It's a welcome mat for the diseased and the fatigued.

It's a God thing.

The Kingdom Breaks In Where Hearts Are Breaking

While the scholars thought the kingdom belonged to the people in the synagogue, Jesus revealed it belonged to people from the streets. There is not a section of society that the kingdom doesn't long to influence and infect. There is no group of people who lie outside kingdom hope or kingdom power, including a woman who had been oppressed and crippled by a spirit for eighteen years.

The kingdom comes in unlikely ways at unlikely times, with unlikely people.

Harry came to faith a couple of years ago. One morning I was speaking at his church and referenced the quote by G. K. Chesterton, "Every man who knocks on the door of a brothel is looking for God." It stood out to Harry because he was an employee at a local strip bar. In that moment, he perceived that the power of the kingdom was present in his workplace and that God had assigned him an environment to transform. The next time I saw Harry, his joy was unmistakable. He told me that numerous people from the strip club had become believers and several had been baptized. He then invited me to pray for one of the girls he had brought to church that morning. Harry was new to faith, but he had just enough faith to continue the ministry of Jesus in an unlikely place with unlikely people.

The kingdom gets everywhere. It breaks into the arts and the media, the skeptic and the atheist, the self-harmer and the addict. The kingdom breaks in where hearts are breaking.

Russell and Vicki were on vacation in Hawaii. It was a time to rest and do what they loved to do. And they loved to reach people with the love of Jesus. They seized every opportunity to explore Hawaii and extend the kingdom. One day Vicki went to the restroom in the hotel and while there sensed the Holy Spirit speak about the lady in the next stall. *She is far from Me, addicted to drugs, and I want you to help her.* Vicki finished her business, then awkwardly hung around in the restroom, pretending to powder her nose while waiting for the lady to emerge. When she did, Vicki greeted her and said, "This will sound a little strange, but I follow Jesus and felt Him say you were struggling with an addiction and He wants to help." The lady broke down, and Vicki prayed for her … in the restroom.

All a little messy. All of it in the hands of scattered servants. Almost like a mustard seed. Or like yeast that a woman took and mixed into about sixty pounds of flour until it worked all through the dough.

The yeast belongs at the heart of the dough just as kingdom power belongs at the heart of communities. When we confine the supernatural to our services, the best we can hope for is renewal. As we release servants who steward the supernatural, we can bring solutions to every corner of culture. We get to see the kingdom break out not only in "ministry times," but *all* the time.

Several years ago, some students from our Encounter School of Mission were learning to speak hope into broken hearts. They would enter coffee shops and not leave until they had given three prophetic words to strangers. As Michelle looked over at a lady, she saw the word *occult* written over her and wondered how to engage her in conversation. (It's not customary to greet someone in our culture with the words, "Hi there, witch.") Eventually she plucked up her courage, approached the lady, and sensing God wanted to meet with her, said, "Don't I know you from somewhere?" As the lady was shaking her head, Michelle added, "Maybe a séance?" The lady explained she had been to a séance before with her sister but would never return as the experience had left both her and her sister emotionally scarred and frightened. Michelle boldly announced, "You need to be set free from your fear—would you mind if we pray for you right now?" The lady agreed and Michelle was able, in the middle of a busy coffee shop, to bring a measure of deliverance into her situation. The following Sunday, both the lady and her sister came to church.

Ryan's Renewal

In his early years, Ryan was plagued by anger issues. He spent much of his childhood in social care and, following his best friend's death, constantly got into fights. He dropped out of school, seeking escape in drugs and self-harm, and was later diagnosed with Borderline Personality Disorder.[14] In his own words, "Drugs couldn't suffocate my anger, and friends couldn't do it. So I joined a gang and started to take it out on others." He spent most of his teenage years in juvenile justice centers or prisons.

Then it seemed like things were changing. He met Sarah, and shortly afterward they were expecting their first child. Ryan was excited to become a father even though everything in life was far from perfect. One night in December, he and Sarah were attending the funeral of Ryan's uncle when a fight broke out in the bar. More than fifteen people were involved and eventually the police were called. One of the police dogs bit Sarah, and Ryan's anger surfaced. In retaliation, he lashed out at one of the officers.

A couple of days later, Ryan was under the influence of drugs again. As he walked through Coleraine town center, a young man named Scott stopped him. He explained the good news of the kingdom but recognized that Ryan wasn't able to process it all in that moment. So Scott invited him to come to a group meeting in his home later that week. Much to his surprise, Ryan came. As he listened, he experienced emotions he didn't know he had. He started crying, then weeping. He fully surrendered his life to Christ, and within the first two weeks of becoming a believer, he and Scott had led twenty-one people to Jesus.

Grace and mercy had invaded Ryan's life ... but his court case was still looming on the horizon. As his day in court approached, our community prayed for leniency but without much expectancy. Ryan's history of being the youngest person to be electronically tagged (and the frequency of his time in prison before) stood against him. He was also in breach of two suspended sentences, which meant it was a certainty he would go to prison for at least six months.

No one expected what happened next, least of all the reporter assigned to cover the court date. Here was the newspaper report:

> A Portstewart man caught up in a pre-Christmas bar brawl in Antrim has made one of the most dramatic changes in lifestyle ever seen by a judge. Lennon had turned his life around and was now being cited as a role model for what young people can do to beat drugs. Mr. Greene said the defendant had a chaotic lifestyle but has been attending church services and is involved with a local church. The Judge said, it is some time since I have seen such a dramatic change in anybody.[15]

Ryan was thankful God had wiped away his past. It was time to enter his future. All he ever wanted was a family. He asked Sarah to marry him and she said yes. Shortly afterward, their beautiful boy, Matthew, was born (and later a second, Levi). Ryan was becoming a family man but still yearning for his birth family to come to Christ. So he quietly got on with his new life while praying for his family, and when opportunity arose, he spoke to them about the goodness and story of God. Slowly each family member turned to Christ.

The transformation in Ryan's life went beyond witnessing to his family; it was reverberating around the community. One Thursday, a couple of our Encounter students were out on the streets. They were stopped by a police officer, who asked if they were part of the church that had been supporting Ryan Lennon. They said yes.

The policeman then said, "Ryan Lennon's transformation has sent ripples throughout the police in Northern Ireland, and they're all talking about the dramatic change." He then said, "You guys will be putting us out of a job soon."

Ryan loved the Encounter students' stories, and it wasn't long before he enrolled in the course. He continued raising his young family while sharing the story of Jesus with others. It wasn't only the events in his life. Everyday moments were kingdom outpourings. In February 2016, he went to a barbershop. Heads were shaved and hearts were shifted as five people found the greatest love of all. Midway through the year, Ryan was invited to share his story at the prestigious Durham University. Seven hundred people crammed into the room as he spoke, and twenty-three of them opened their lives to Christ for the first time.

Ryan is inscribing hope everywhere he goes, especially in the lives of young people who have similar stories to his. It hasn't gone unnoticed by the police or the Prince of Wales. Another news account said:

> An inspirational Portstewart man, who turned his life around after seeking solace in drugs and self-harm, has been honoured by the Prince's Trust. Ryan Lennon, who ended up behind bars, now gives talks to inmates and helps others battling addictions and homelessness. The 22-year-old won the Devenish Rising Star Award during a ceremony held in Titanic Belfast last week recognising the achievements of disadvantaged young people who

have succeeded against the odds, improved their chances in life and had a positive impact on their local community.[16]

Almost three years since his last brush with the law, Ryan was looking at a return to prison once again. Only this time to lead the Alpha course. Ryan spent years avoiding community or destroying community but is now bringing life to the city. His sense is that God is speaking over the city, saying, "I will change disconnection to connection, and lack of trust to infinite love." It's beginning to happen. In the last few months, all of Ryan's closest friends from his teenage years have come to church, and every one of them has made a commitment to Christ.

Ryan says, "Six years ago I got sentenced to three years for supplying drugs. This year I graduated, got employed, and moved into a new family home in August."

It's the kingdom, and when it gets loose in a life, it gets everywhere!

Refusing to Settle for Less

This is what happens when the church leaves the building—the presence of Jesus comes in power! Power to change lives. Power to set people free. Power to clothe them in their right mind. Power to make a difference wherever scattered servants like you go. When we broaden our awareness of who the kingdom is for, we can't stand for the kingdom not to be around.

We can't settle for a life without …

> Seeing holiness of heart and life.
> Seeing the poor receive good news.
> Seeing the brokenhearted heal.
> Seeing the lonely find families.
> Seeing the Scriptures taught in a life-giving way.
> Seeing people released to discover God and say yes to Him.

We can't settle for life the way it was or the way it's always been.

It is normal for those who live under the *influence* of the Spirit of God to live in an *increase* of the power of God. Our Father wants to take us beyond encountering the supernatural and into enlargement. Actually establishing that thing in us. He wants to give us our inheritance. And the inheritance is always greater than the experience. Experience you can get immediately, but inheritance always requires process and patience. We'll discuss that in the pages ahead.

Chapter 9

KINGDOM CARRIERS WHO STEWARD THE SUPERNATURAL

Every day is a day of encounter. Every day is designed to be a day of kingdom advancement.[1] We are seeing it, and we are increasingly seeing it.

But there was a time when we didn't. More accurately, there was a time when we didn't know how to grow in the power of the Holy Spirit. We thought it sovereignly landed on you or it didn't. And while we sensed it was possible to partner with the Holy Spirit to continue the ministry of Jesus, we didn't know how to do so. We didn't know how to move from sporadic intervention to sustained inheritance. We didn't know how to move from seeing power, into seasons of power, and then into being sustained by power.

So we attended gatherings, had wonderful experiences, became skilled at receiving power—but we didn't know how to release power. We didn't know how to make the exceptional moments everyday, normal moments. How to *live in* ongoing outpouring. And we are living in days of outpouring! As the writer of Acts assured us, "[Jesus is] exalted to the right hand of God, [and] he has received from the Father the promised Holy Spirit and has poured out what you now see and hear."[2]

As long as Jesus is still exalted, we are set up for increasing encounter. As long as Jesus is still above every name, we can expect to see every knee bow. As long as Jesus reigns over all, we can expect outpouring for all. And we can expect *ongoing* outpouring for all. This is the thinking behind Luke's earlier phrase, "All that Jesus began to do and teach."[3] The word *began* implies that Jesus started something and isn't finished yet. He is still working among us.

Although the book of Acts records incredible stories of the Holy Spirit at work in power, it was only supposed to be the beginning. It was never intended to be the high-water mark. It's designed to fuel in us a hunger for more. We are designed to read it, then release it. Come under its influence, then have the experience. Their exceptional moments are supposed to become our everyday moments. It is normal for those who live under the influence of the Spirit of God to live in an increase of the power of God.

Growing in the Supernatural

So why don't we see more? It's a great question. And it's one that I have wrestled with personally and one that I am asked frequently.

Indeed, one of the questions I am asked most frequently is, "Why do you think you (and your church) see *so much* healing on the streets?" Sometimes those asking the question want to attribute it to gifting. Other times they ask with a desire to find a way that they can see the same thing where they live. Whatever the reason for the question, my answer is always the same …

Stewardship. The kingdom comes in moments, and through faithful stewardship, increases in increments until it transforms environments.[4]

Stewardship is the intentional process whereby we learn to increase and expand what God has entrusted to us. When we learn to steward the supernatural, we *do* see more—more healing, more breakthroughs, more provision, and more moments of awe. Additionally, we progressively "become the kind of person who routinely practices the words and works of Jesus" with a rhythm and routine that releases increase.[5]

However, increase doesn't just land on you—you steward it. You don't get a download of increase. You develop it. Growing in kingdom power, like all aspects of spiritual growth, is neither automatic nor sporadic. Neither is it formulaic. It is intentional. It requires faithfulness with what we have been given by grace, combined with focus. So at Causeway Coast Vineyard, we learned to value what we had been given. Then intentionally invested it, while asking the question, "Is our investment expanding? Is it multiplying the initial deposit we had been given?"

Treasure it. Try it. Think about it. Think about how to do it again or differently next time.

Stewardship is the process whereby we *learn* to increase and expand what God has entrusted to us.

"So how do we steward the supernatural?" I'm glad I asked.

Stewarding the Supernatural

Like financial stewardship, stewarding the supernatural requires discipline, cultivation, and intentional focus. While the church has given significant attention to financial stewardship, we have largely neglected our responsibility to steward the supernatural. Yet Jesus made it clear that financial stewardship—handling earthly resources—is a test for being trusted with kingdom reality. "So if you have not been trustworthy in handling worldly wealth, who will trust you with true riches?"[6] The purpose of learning to handle the wealth of this world is to learn the process for handling the wealth of His world. We are called to steward the supernatural realities of the kingdom.

Again, when we steward the supernatural, we live our lives in such a way that expectation and expansion of the grace of God occurs in our lives. This was common practice in the New Testament. So much so that Peter instructed the church to grow in grace, assuming they understood what that meant and would know when that happened. I am not suggesting that kingdom power is the prism for understanding grace, but it's often present when grace grows in a life. "With great power the apostles continued to testify to the resurrection of the Lord Jesus. And God's grace was so powerfully at work in them all."[7] This "much grace" indicated increase in what they had originally been given. Yet it did not happen spontaneously. It happened gradually as the apostles determined not to live on the same level they had previously.

How do we get to the place where great power and much grace are upon us all?

How do we continue to testify to the resurrection among the people?

How do we get to the place where more and more people are being healed?

How do we sustain existing breakthrough and succeed in breaking through to even greater things?

Exactly the same way we do in any area of spiritual formation. We grow through understanding what we have received and intentionally focusing on becoming better stewards.

Stewarding versus Safeguarding

When Jesus told stories about the kingdom, He didn't tell stories about sudden invasion of the kingdom. He talked about gradual increase of the kingdom. Perhaps His most famous stewardship talk appears in Luke 19:11–26:

> While they were listening to this, he went on to tell them a parable, because he was near Jerusalem and the people thought that the kingdom of God was going to appear at once. He said: "A man of noble birth went to a distant country to have himself appointed king and then to return. So he called ten of his servants and gave them ten minas. 'Put this money to work,' he said, 'until I come back.'

"But his subjects hated him and sent a delegation after him to say, 'We don't want this man to be our king.'

"He was made king, however, and returned home. Then he sent for the servants to whom he had given the money, in order to find out what they had gained with it.

"The first one came and said, 'Sir, your mina has earned ten more.'

"'Well done, my good servant!' his master replied. 'Because you have been trustworthy in a very small matter, take charge of ten cities.'

"The second came and said, 'Sir, your mina has earned five more.'

"His master answered, 'You take charge of five cities.'

"Then another servant came and said, 'Sir, here is your mina; I have kept it laid away in a piece of cloth. I was afraid of you, because you are a hard man. You take out what you did not put in and reap what you did not sow.'

"His master replied, 'I will judge you by your own words, you wicked servant! You knew, did you, that I am a hard man, taking out what I did not put in, and reaping what I did not sow? Why then didn't you put my money on deposit, so that when I came back, I could have collected it with interest?'

"Then he said to those standing by, 'Take his mina away from him and give it to the one who has ten minas.'

"'Sir,' they said, 'he already has ten!'

"He replied, 'I tell you that to everyone who has, more will be given, but as for the one who has nothing, even what they have will be taken away.'"

The wicked servant safeguarded what he had been given. The wise servant stewarded it. Stewarding is different than safeguarding.

In safeguarding, accountability looks like avoiding failure. I make sure the entrustment doesn't die on my watch. In stewarding, however, I am responsible for advancing the entrustment. I become a good steward when the things entrusted to me get multiplied through my hands. With this mind-set, accountability looks like increasing … even multiplying favor. Stewarding is the process of managing abundance until it becomes our inheritance. I take what I have inherited, what I have been given, and work it into my life. I put it to work, so that increase is the result. The initial outpouring becomes the source of ongoing abundance.

The supernatural was never intended to be seasonal. It was intended to be stewarded.

More Than Observers

It's not enough to see what God is doing when our privilege is to steward what God is doing. As a scattered servant, you weren't designed to be an observer of the kingdom; you were called to be an ambassador or broker of the kingdom.

At Causeway Coast Vineyard we used to observe supernatural encounters on the streets or in church and wonder how they had happened. We were amazed at the goodness of God. But amazement doesn't increase faith. Engagement does. God is not seeking people who are *amazed* at what He *can* do; He is looking for people who will *engage* with what He *is* doing. Many times people in the Bible would gather around what God was doing, yet walk away unchanged. Consider Mark 6:46–52:

> After leaving them, he went up on a mountainside to pray. Later that night, the boat was in the middle of the lake, and he was alone on land. He saw the disciples straining at the oars, because the wind was against them. Shortly before dawn he went out to them, walking on the lake. He was about to pass by them, but when they saw him walking on the lake, they thought he was a ghost. They cried out, because they all saw him and were terrified. Immediately he spoke to them and said, "Take courage! It is I. Don't be afraid." Then he climbed into the boat with them, and the wind died down. They were completely amazed, for they had not understood about the loaves; their hearts were hardened.

Seeing the miraculous without engaging in the stewardship process actually hardens our hearts. The disciples' amazement reflected their inner reality. It revealed that their hearts had not been penetrated by the miraculous sufficiently for their minds to be transformed. Later, the very same disciples would realize their folly and rebuke others for their amazement. As we read in Acts 3:9–12:

> When all the people saw him walking and praising God, they recognized him as the same man who used to sit begging at the temple gate called Beautiful, and they were filled with wonder and amazement at what had happened to him. While the man held on to Peter and John, all the people were astonished and came running to them in the place called Solomon's Colonnade. When Peter saw this, he said to them: "Fellow Israelites, why does this surprise you?"

It is entirely possible to be in the middle of a miraculous movement of God, marveling at His power, yet miss the requirement of faith. When this happens, it creates a barrier to increase. Amazement is not engagement, and amazement is not faith.

Stewardship moves us from watching God at work to working with God. And in order to create a supernatural culture, we have to move on from watching God at work, walking away, and then waiting on the next time. Such behavior does not produce a biblically supernatural lifestyle. At best it might furnish an occasionally supernatural lifestyle. Yet our communities need more and deserve better. We have an obligation to walk in the power of the Holy Spirit before a watching world.[8]

Intensity Doesn't Create Increase— Insight Does

As a young believer I thought intensity was the gateway to increase. I read the Scripture "eagerly [desiring] spiritual gifts"[9] so I earnestly and intensely pursued them. I prayed and fasted, read books, consulted mentors, received prayers of intercession and impartation. All of which is commendable, even biblical. But in my endeavors to grow, I missed one vital component: increase comes from God's generosity, not my intensity.

Increase comes as I recognize what I have already been given. Let's unpack this again through the Scripture we referenced earlier. "For whoever has, to him more shall be given, and he will have an abundance."[10] What is Jesus saying? I think He is saying, "The one who gets it grows in it."

What do you see?

Some see fruit. Some see an apple. Some see an apple tree. Some see an orchard.

Everyone who holds an apple carries an orchard in their hands, *if* they know what they have. You can't grow what you have until you know what you have. You must have insight. Therefore, insight is the forerunner to increase. Insight leads to increase. The Bible tells us that God has blessed us with every spiritual blessing in the heavenly realms.[11] Everything you need to live a supernatural lifestyle is already *in* your life. We don't need more impartation—we need more insight into what we already have.

Insight makes the difference. It helps us recognize the goodness of God, so we can release the goodness of God everywhere. Without insight, there are incidents of the supernatural but they are unsustained; we have waves and moves of God but little breakthrough or momentum. Without insight we *move* in the miraculous, but fail to *live* in it. Insight creates and generates increasing capacity to live a supernatural lifestyle. It sets us up for a life of sustained interaction rather than sporadic intervention.

See It, Do It, Understand It

Since insight is at the core of kingdom activity, it is imperative to gain insight. How do we gain insight? Through reflection. Paul writes to Timothy, "Reflect on these things and the Lord will give you insight."[12]

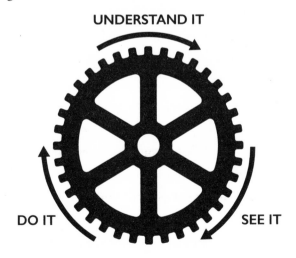

At Causeway Coast Vineyard, we used to see the kingdom occasionally but not consistently because we didn't understand it. We used to see it in our services but not in our servants because we didn't understand it. We used to see it in seasons, sporadically rather than continuously, because we didn't understand it. We had no grid for processing the supernatural.

In order to engage effectively with what the Father is doing, we need to be able to see. Jesus said, "I only do what I see my Father doing."[13] Sometimes He saw in the moment; other times Jesus saw from a place of momentum. We need to see what the Father is doing *and* see what He has already given.

Speaking to Nathaniel, Jesus said, "You believe because I saw you. What's going to happen in your faith when you see heaven opened?" Seeing the supernatural is the key to stewarding. We have to recognize what our Father is doing.

See it	Do it	Understand it cycle
Recognize	Release	Reflect

You can enter the cycle at any point and begin stewarding. The key to continuous growth is to go through each phase at some point. Perhaps you read something in Scripture and have an understanding of its reality before you ever see it in your own life or release it into the lives of others. Likewise, you may have an encounter or experience that you know is authentic, but you don't yet have an explanation. You can enter the cycle at any point.

While God often gives us things before we understand them, they only grow in our lives through understanding. When we fail to understand what the Father is doing, it gets wasted in our lives.[14] The life of another world has to be combined with understanding if it is to bear fruit. While we can't limit our encounters merely to what we can understand, we grow in depth and frequency of encounter through understanding.

The Big Is in the Small: Recognizing What We Have

Many of us miss what we have because it doesn't look like much. We forget that you don't have to get it all at once. It can grow! As a result we often look for big events and big moments. However, those with insight refuse to confuse the dramatic—that which is amazing in the moment and attracts attention—with the dynamic. The dynamic is the small thing that contains the seed of movement and acceleration within it.

We see so many things that don't look amazing at the time. It's because God hides the big in the small. As the prophet Zechariah said, "Do not despise this small beginning, for the eyes of the Lord rejoice to see the work begin."[15]

God often starts small and then works with our faith to bring about increase. If we are going to steward the supernatural and release the kingdom wherever we are, we must focus on what we have been given, not what is missing. God starts small and then works with our faith to bring about increase. Therefore, rejoice in the small. Rejoice in it even though you long to see more.

The Awesome Is in the Awkward: Raising the Bar of Risk

In stewarding the supernatural, we recognize that the awesome is in the awkward. Some of Jesus' most amazing healings were surrounded by awkwardness. Highlighting a man's disability in front of everyone is *awkward*.[16] Drawing attention to a lady who had an issue of blood is *awkward*.[17] Spitting and putting mud on someone's eyes is *awkward*.[18] I have discovered that I am not very good at being naturally supernatural, but I'm really good at being awkwardly supernatural. And I am grateful that God hides the awesome in the awkward.

He often invites us to reach beyond the comfortable in order to receive the supernatural. We learn to operate in increased authority through intentionally embracing greater vulnerability. We deliberately raise the bar of risk when it looks like nothing is happening, and sometimes when others are questioning what is already happening.

The Fruit Is Where You Feel the Fear: Release the Kingdom to Others

The psalmist declared, "You prepare a table before me in the presence of my enemies."[19] There are some things God has for us that are only available in the presence of enemies. Fear is often the signal that God is about to increase your fruitfulness.

I call it the scarecrow principle. Scarecrows are strategically positioned in the field to deter those who want to go after the fruit. Scarecrows are incapable of preventing crows from picking up the fruit because they are immobile. Their only hope is to intimidate crows out of their fruit. Scarecrows only work because crows are dumb. Yet to a smart crow, a scarecrow is an advertisement. Every time it sees a scarecrow it knows to venture into that field because that is where the greatest fruitfulness is available and possible.

Fear is like a scarecrow. It seeks to intimidate you out of your inheritance.

Yet for insightful believers, fear is the indicator that there is fruit in the field. Resist the temptation to sacrifice your future on the altar of fear. Properly faced, fear can become a doorway to favor. Hostility can become the training ground for authority. Indeed, hostility represents the invitation to exercise greater authority. As you step out in the supernatural, don't be surprised at the impossibility you are facing. Don't be anxious if you feel afraid. The Father is setting you up to see greater things. God always prepares a table in the presence of your enemies.

Momentum Is in the Moment: Repeat the Process

In stewarding the supernatural, we learn that every moment carries momentum. If you see it once, it's yours from then on. Often we assume that the first time we see breakthrough is an exception, and that we will probably never see or experience it again. As a result, we fail to allow it to govern our expectation. But once we have insight that momentum is in the moment, a new normal begins to govern our hearts. We realize this is going to be normal from this point forward. It may still require wrestling and contending until they occur in our lives and streets with increasing regularity. However, we no longer have to live with lack in that area of our lives. Moses understood this reality:

> Next we turned and went up along the road toward Bashan, and Og king of Bashan with his whole army marched out to meet us in battle at Edrei. The LORD said to me, "Do not be afraid of him, for I have delivered him into your hands, along with his whole army and his land. Do to him what you did to Sihon king of the Amorites, who reigned in Heshbon." So the LORD our God also gave into our hands Og king of Bashan and all his army.... At that time I commanded Joshua: "You have seen with your own eyes all that the LORD your God has done to these two kings. The LORD will do the same to all the kingdoms over there where you are going."[20]

Moses is essentially saying, "Your history is the signpost to your inheritance in this area. As you take the memory of previous victory into new territory, your one-off experience becomes the doorway to ongoing abundance. Now that you have seen God move this way once, it's yours from then on." Since most of us don't have a Moses speaking into our breakthrough moments, we miss their import for other moments. We celebrate what God has done but fail to integrate it.

Still, to the person who has one breakthrough moment, many more will be given. If you see one healing, God wants to give you more. If you see one person set free from addiction, God wants to give you more. If you see one church planted, God wants to give you more. Scattered servants know that one moment in the supernatural is a seed that creates a future for a movement in the supernatural.

The Invitation for a Lifetime

When God gives us a glimpse of His work, He does so inviting us to experience that work *in* our lifetime, *for* our lifetime. In the past, we viewed moments of initial breakthrough as phenomena rather than paradigms. Phenomena are rare moments, perhaps once-in-a-lifetime moments. Paradigms are moments that frame a lifetime. Learn to capture the momentum in the moment and know that when you see it once, you have just been handed the permission to see so much more where that came from. Learn to increasingly anticipate and operate in that realm. And as you do, you will regularly see the power of God

Our church was inspired by the story of To Write Love on Her Arms (TWLOHA), a nonprofit organization that brings hope and healing to people struggling with addiction, depression, self-injury, and suicidal thoughts. So we began addressing issues of self-harm in our community. We highlighted the issue with our teens and partnered with our community to counsel those struggling with self-harm. In the process we witnessed some beautiful recovery and restoration. Yet while the psychological scars were slowly removed, the physical scars from cutting remained. It prompted our youth pastor to pray for breakthrough. She had never seen or heard of scars disappearing before, but she had to reach for more.

One night she reached out her hands to pray for one of our young folks who had significant scarring. It didn't happen right away. But each time she prayed, the scars reduced, slowly new tissue formed, and by the fourth prayer there was no sign of scarring on the arms. This was more than a scar disappearing. It was a new story beginning. It was the sign and the seal of divine adoption. It was beautiful.

And it would have been a great story even if that's where it ended.

But because we already knew how to steward it, the moment brought significant momentum. We had seen it once and knew God would do the same with other scarred lives. The girl whose scars disappeared was having coffee one summer's day when a stranger literally bumped into her—spilling her coffee. After a brief conversation, she noticed that the lady was wearing a long-sleeve top and so sensitively asked if she self-harmed. The lady rolled up her sleeves. Filled with expectancy, the girl from our youth group asked if she could take a photo of the scars so they would have a "before and after prayer" visual. The lady agreed. So they prayed and the scars dissolved. The one who had been a victim of self-harming was now vanquishing it in the lives of others. It was a stunning picture of the kingdom.

And it would be a great story even if that's where the story ended.

The girl sent the photos to the youth pastor who had prayed for her and also showed them to a vicar from Dublin. The following Sunday at his church, he told the story of the scars disappearing and showed the photos on screen. At the service was a sixteen-year-old girl who had been self-harming by cutting her own stomach. Later that afternoon as she was changing her clothes, she noticed that every one of the scars on her stomach had completely disappeared.

Well, now we weren't just seeing scars disappear *after* prayer, but we were also seeing scars disappear *without* prayer.

I told the story in our church. A few weeks later, I was scheduled to speak at a conference in New Zealand. Without my knowledge, one of the local radio stations in the city played the short clip of me telling the story to our congregation. As the story from the radio station was broadcast in one of the churches attending the conference, a man in the congregation addicted to heroin for many years tried to get the attention of the leader. He would look at the leader and then look at his arm. Now all the signs of his addiction were gone. He still had one scar on his wrist, but it was from an accident when he was a kid. This event was about more than a scar disappearing; it was about wholeness coming to a man whose addiction had been his life story—but no more. Today a new story of wholeness surfaced in his arms for all to see.

Momentum was growing. Now it wasn't just scars from cutting, but also scars from addiction being healed.

It was time to risk more. So as I stood at a conference in Southampton, I invited anyone who had scars for any reason to stand. While I prayed for thirty seconds from the front, people gathered around those standing and began to pray. When we asked those standing to check for improvements, scars were being healed all over the room. It was remarkable. As other healings were occurring, I continued to say, "Try doing something you couldn't do before, if it's appropriate." Faith surged in the heart of a lady who had undergone a hysterectomy six months previously. She began to wonder if God might have moved on her body. She promptly went to the bathroom to check. As she did, she saw that 80 percent of the scar had disappeared and watched as the remainder vanished. It was more than a scar disappearing; it was wholeness coming to a woman who felt less of a woman because of her operation. But now she had the assurance of God's presence no matter what life took from her.

As I told these stories recently at a leaders conference, a woman was present who really wasn't sure she should be there. Her daughter was at home in the grip of depression and really didn't want her mum to leave. She had spent some time as a self-harmer. Upon hearing the stories of wholeness, the lady texted her daughter to say it was possible for scars to disappear. Since the daughter's phone was charging, she didn't get the message immediately. When she did, she looked down at her leg and noticed that all the scars were gone in one leg and the word *worthless,* which she had etched into her leg, had been swallowed up by wholeness. Completely clean. It was more than a scar disappearing; it was a teenager and a mother feeling hope again for the future and finding their relationship restored.

None of it would have happened had we not learned to steward the supernatural.

Chapter 10

AUTHORITY TO CHANGE THE STORY OF YOUR COMMUNITY

Although young, they were relatively experienced church leaders. She was the primary worship leader of a megachurch particularly effective at engaging millennials. He was responsible for helping those in the church and leaders from others churches increase their capacity in ministering prayer. And yet both hungered for more. They knew how to gather people, how to grow ministries, and how to present and preach in a way that increased attendance. Yet neither of them understood or were aware of the authority residing on their lives.

With that in mind, they asked if they could intern with us for nine months.

Not long after arriving in our community, they moved beyond the building. It was unfamiliar terrain for them. But it woke them.

Authority latent within them came alive. Enlivened, they engaged all the more, risking and reaching for the kingdom at every opportunity. And then the stories started to surface—stories of lost people coming to faith, of sick people being healed, of lives being restored. The young couple who knew how to develop church ministry had discovered how to release kingdom authority. It changed them. It changed everything.

They returned home intent on planting a church that blessed the city. They were going beyond recruiting volunteers; they were going to raise up trusted rulers.

Raised Up to Lead

Trusted rulers are believers who bring life to cities. They know their identity, understand their spiritual authority, and use *that* authority to bring life to the city.

Paul's first words to the church in Ephesus provide a stunning example of the mind-set of a trusted ruler:

> Paul, an apostle of Christ Jesus by the will of God, to God's holy people in Ephesus, the faithful in Christ Jesus: Grace and peace to you from God our Father and the Lord Jesus Christ. Praise be to the God and Father of our Lord Jesus Christ, who has blessed us in the heavenly realms with every spiritual blessing in Christ.[1]

It's clear Paul is no longer living out his old identity. No longer imprisoned by his past. He is Paul, not Saul. He knows his identity and authority in Christ. He writes as *an apostle*—someone given authority from heaven to change the culture on earth. The word *apostle* simply means *sent one*; sent with a mandate to introduce new possibilities and capacities into every sphere of humanity. He writes "to the saints in Ephesus," those who are treasured and held in high honor. His choice of words reminds them of their new identity in Christ, who they are in Christ. And then he reminds them of what they have in Christ. God has blessed them with every spiritual blessing and given them authority. Paul begins this letter this way because he knows that believers who know who they are and what they carry bring life to the city.

His emphasis is on their sonship, not their services. His emphasis is on changing culture, not church structure. It's the mind-set that governs all of our models at Causeway Coast Vineyard. But it never used to be. We used to operate with a skilled supportive servant model/mind-set.

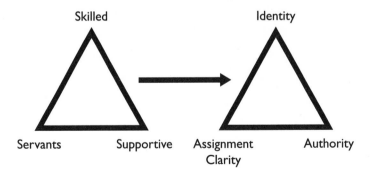

The triangle on the left represents skilled supportive servants. It's what we dreamed of when we planted Causeway Coast Vineyard.[2] We weren't alone. It's the normal model for church life. Every church pastor and planter dreams of skilled supportive servants. People who buy into the vision, people who are behind you as a leader, people who step out and serve, and people who work hard to bring their skills to the table. If you get enough skilled supportive servants, you can build a great gathered environment, have stunning services, and exceptional programs.

But there was a problem with our thinking. Actually lots of problems ...

We were using people to build church instead of growing people who changed culture.

We were succeeding in growing church structures but failing to raise sons and daughters.

We were recruiting good volunteers instead of releasing trusted rulers.[3]

Nothing in our model of "doing church" required believers to know their identity. None of it empowered believers to understand their spiritual authority. And none of it engaged believers in their assignment of bringing change to the surrounding culture. In short, all of it failed to unleash the power of everyone, everywhere.

So we gradually changed the paradigm from skilled supportive servants and leaned toward helping believers know their royal identity as sons and daughters of God. Treasured by Him. A royal priesthood, a holy nation. Heirs and co-heirs with Christ. When we sensed people were serving at our weekend services from a root of shame, we asked them to stop serving until they were secure in their identity. Ministry was intended to be the overflow of identity, not the gateway to identity.

We also began teaching people their kingdom authority. Our lives were designed to carry heaven's authority. We are ambassadors and reconcilers of all of creation. Our ministry isn't to support church. Our ministry is to shape culture. We don't need to occupy a position in church. God has already given us all things in Christ. Therefore, at Causeway Coast Vineyard it became more important that believers exercise authority within their regular environments than attend church events.[4] Our bold goal was that every believer know their adoption, authority, and assignment. And then begin to shape the community through their story.

This was God's intention all along. "His intent was that now, through the church, the manifold wisdom of God should be made known to the rulers and authorities in the heavenly realms."[5]

A Community with Authority

The word *church* (*ekklesia*) is intentionally selected by Jesus to describe the community that lives for the Father and leads the earth into life. It's a borrowed term, frequently used to describe a community that had been called out of ordinary life, gathered together for the purpose of influencing the city, and given authority to bring about change in the city. Therefore, understanding and exercising authority is integral to the essence of church.

Until the church learns to exercise authority among the people, she hasn't fully understood her identity or her role in society. She preserves an institution on earth instead of demonstrating intervention from heaven. In truth, without authority, we don't have a church; we have a gathering. While gatherings can be fun, they don't bring life to the city. It's insufficient to gather at weekend services to hear teaching without impartation. It's insufficient to show people how to serve *in* church rather than serve *as* church. It's insufficient to have church activity without kingdom authority.

Structural authority *is* vital. But it doesn't work outside the structure. Spiritual authority is viral. It operates everywhere in culture. Not every believer has structural authority, but every believer has spiritual authority. Kingdom authority isn't reserved for certain professions or locations. Kingdom authority is for everything everywhere. The church leader has authority and the street sweeper has authority. The executive pastor has authority and the barista has authority. Not every believer has authority *in* the church, but every believer has authority *as* the church.

Scattered servants embody a movement of people empowered by the Holy Spirit and sent to bring life to the city. The intention of Jesus was to have a people capable of bringing change to any and every city. In order for this to happen, He gave them authority:

> Jesus called his twelve disciples to him and gave them authority to drive out impure spirits and to heal every disease and sickness.... These twelve Jesus sent out with the following instructions: "Do not go among the Gentiles or enter any town of the Samaritans. Go rather to the lost sheep of Israel. As you go, proclaim this message: 'The kingdom of heaven has come near.' Heal the sick, raise the dead, cleanse those who have leprosy, drive out demons. Freely you have received; freely give."[6]

Jesus knew that when the church shows up and shares, society shifts. Kingdom authority is for the streets, not just for the priests.

Ministry Strategy Is a Poor Substitute for Kingdom Authority

We have been content to exercise structural authority to change church structures, when Christ has called us to exercise spiritual authority to change culture. Instead of allowing His authority to be the catalytic dynamic at the heart of mission and spiritual formation, we have limited what He can do to what we can do. And ministry strategy is a poor substitute for kingdom authority.

We exercise enormous energy devising ways of increasing *attendance* of our churches while giving scant attention to *awakening* and unlocking the latent *authority* within our churches. Consequently, we have developed programs to reach the city, instead of becoming people who release the city. I get it. As a young church planter, I focused upon strategies for creating larger gatherings in the hope that our city might notice and with the equation brimming in my heart that substantial size leads to greater influence with the city.

While strategies are birthed with noble intention and are widespread, they are limited. Strategy can deliver bigger churches, but it is powerless to deliver broken cities. Only kingdom authority can make that happen.

Little wonder Jesus operated with a different mind-set and methodology. He rarely spoke of the size of attendance, and on the few occasions He referenced size, it related to the significance of the small.[7] Jesus drew attention to the substance of His presence actively and gloriously among us. "For where two or three gather in my name, there I am with them."[8] Jesus knew what we often forget: the attendance of our gathering is immaterial; the authority resting on our lives in inconceivable.

Scattered Servants Carry Unusual Authority

Tom came to faith a few years ago. He encountered the kingdom as God healed his body on the streets. It was enough to recalibrate his heart, and at the age of eighty-one, Tom believed.

A year later, Tom applied for our Encounter School of Mission. When I heard he had applied, I was surprised. The course is specifically designed to create a climate of risk. Upon reflection, I realized that, although it was a little late for a gap year, Tom was perfectly positioned to live a life of risk. At his age, there weren't many people who didn't know Tom in our town. He had already established a fine reputation. He had a lot to lose.

Yet he embraced the risk and stepped into learning again. He started the course in September with one goal: to lead someone to Jesus. In February 2014, God granted Tom the desire of his heart. Within a year Tom led twenty-four people to Jesus, and also had the privilege of joining Jesus in leading his seventy-nine-year-old brother to life.

After he finished the course, Tom continued to risk the impossible. Here is one of his authority adventures:

> We went to the train station this morning. There
> was a women standing outside having a cigarette,

so we asked her if there was anything we could pray for her. She said she had too many troubles to mention, but would like prayer. After we prayed, I asked her what had happened during prayer. She said she experienced incredible peace and had never felt anything like it before. We then shared the kingdom message of Jesus and she asked Him into her life.

Another girl was standing nearby. So we asked if there was anything for which she needed prayer. She said she had a very sore stomach. Again we prayed, and the Holy Spirit came upon her in power and completely healed her. She said, "I have no pain now at all." So we went next door to the market, where we saw a woman using a Zimmer frame [a walker]. As usual we asked her if she needed prayer for anything. She said she was crippled with pain. So we prayed and God showed up and filled her. We shared the message of King Jesus with her and she asked Him into her life.

At eighty-one years old, we could have made Tom an usher in our services, but he was too busy ushering in the kingdom on our streets. Tom isn't just getting old. Tom is growing old. Tom discovered his authority and in the process found his own story late in the journey. Everyone is sent. And everyone has authority.

You. Have. Authority.

You may not see it or feel it, but you have it. Every believer does. Kingdom authority is given to every follower to bring everything everywhere into alignment with the agenda of the King. You are seated together with Christ and raised up with Him over the principalities and powers, over demons and disease. Uncommon authority rests on your life.

You have unusual authority, but you do not have unlimited authority. That is reserved for the Name Above All Names, the King before whom every knee must bow and every tongue confess. It is the domain of He "who must reign until all His enemies are made His footstool."[9] Jesus Christ is the supreme majesty and ruler of the kings of the earth.

It is important to remember, therefore, that spiritual authority does not originate with you or in you. All authority comes from and belongs to Christ. He is the rightful ruler over all things, the King of Kings and Lord of Lords. And so every other authority is a secondary authority, a delegated authority.[10] Since our authority is delegated, we dare not use it simply to exert our own desires or preferences. We refuse to use our authority according to the pattern of the world around us where people throw their weight around. Nonetheless, the abuse of authority by others is not an excuse for us to not use the authority God entrusted to us.

When Will You Use Your Authority?

John Wimber, the pioneer and former leader of the Vineyard Movement of Churches, was an excellent musician and businessman who, after his conversion to Christ (through the ministry of the Friends Church), became a church consultant. Primarily he traveled throughout the United States and other parts of the world helping churches optimize their potential for growth. His official title was a "church growth consultant." Not surprisingly, given his business acumen and brilliance in exegeting culture, many of the churches he worked with experienced an upsurge in attendance, placing even greater travel and time demands upon John. On the outside it looked like Wimber was fulfilling his ministry, yet on the inside something was missing.

Several years into his role, Wimber attended a conference that would change everything. During the course of the conference, a lady approached him and announced that God had given her a prophetic word for him. She said, "God wants to know when you are going to use your authority." John freely admitted he didn't know what authority the lady was referring to. He didn't know he had authority.

Although John had an unusual ability, he hadn't yet learned to exercise spiritual authority. But as he stepped into his authority, he stepped into his destiny. He didn't know at the time that stepping into his authority would change his story—and rewrite the story of many others. His personal discovery of exercising spiritual authority became a source of renewal and spiritual awakening for many churches across the world.[11] John awakened to his authority, and it brought life to his church and community.

You have authority to change the story. And God wants to know when you are going to use your authority.

Awakening to the Authority Adventure

The Ephesian church was birthed in miraculous authority. Their first steps in faith were spent breathing in the miraculous presence and goodness of God. Although they had witnessed God at work, it seems they became more conscious of the powers around them than the power within them. So, much of Paul's letter to the Ephesians was written to remind them of Christ's supremacy and authority over the powers.

He also spent significant time reminding them that Christ's authority meant they also had authority.

> I pray that the eyes of your heart may be enlightened in order that you may know the hope to which he has called you, the riches of his glorious inheritance in his holy people, and his incomparably great power for us who believe. That power is the same as the mighty strength he exerted when he raised Christ from the dead and seated him at his right hand in the heavenly realms, far above all rule and authority, power and dominion, and every name that is invoked, not only in the present age but also in the one to come. And God placed all things under his feet and appointed him to be head over everything for the church, which is his body, the fullness of him who fills everything in every way.[12]

He continues: "And God raised us up with Christ and seated us with him in the heavenly realms in Christ Jesus."[13] He raised us up far above all rule and authority, power and dominion. He raised us up to rest in God's presence and reign in His righteousness.[14]

Paul's point is that God's unique grace *toward* us unlocks uncommon authority *in* us. That is to say that people who understand grace fully live with unusual kingdom authority. You are *saved* by grace, and you have been *raised* by grace. By grace you have been raised to a position of influence. Therefore, *you* are a person of influence, destined to rule and reign in life.[15] This has been God's desire all along. God's intention has always been that your life becomes a reference point of His grace and glory. *You are to be the shop window for the resources of heaven.* Your life is meant to demonstrate the impossible, the inexplicable, and the radical kindness of God in this world.

Grace doesn't only cover your failure; it also opens your future and the future of others. Amazing grace brought you into a place of astonishing authority. But it can be difficult to detect, so it often lies dormant. That's why Paul writes, "Wake up, sleeper, rise from the dead, and Christ will shine on you."[16] It seems the Ephesians had been asleep to the authority adventure.

Revivalist Leonard Ravenhill perceptively captures the sleeping church when recounting the following story:

> Solemnly and slowly, with his index finger extended, Napoleon Bonaparte outlined a great stretch of country on a map of the world. "There," he growled, "is a sleeping giant. Let him sleep! If he wakes, he will shake the world." That sleeping giant was China. Today, Bonaparte's prophecy of some one hundred and fifty years ago makes sense. Today, Lucifer is probably surveying the church just as Bonaparte did China. One can almost behold the fear in his eyes as he thinks of the church's unmeasured potential and growls, "Let the church

sleep! If she wakes, she will shake the world." Is not
the church the sleeping giant of today?[17]

It's time for awakening. It's time to shift our focus from creating
irresistible services in our churches and raise up unstoppable servants
who carry kingdom authority into every activity. It's time for us to
awaken to the authority adventure.

It was wonderful to watch this happen a few years ago on the
streets of St. Andrews.

This city sits on the east coast of my home nation, Scotland, and
it's known for its university and for the Royal and Ancient Golf Club.
But it wasn't always so. St. Andrews was once ground zero for faith
in the nation, an epicenter of vibrant spirituality. It's grand cathedral
dominated the landscape of ecclesiastical life for centuries. Then came
the birth pangs of the Scottish Reformation, when the martyrdom of
first Patrick Hamilton and then George Wishart in the city ignited the
fires of reformation, which spread throughout the country.

Today the cathedral is no longer habitable, and the once vibrant
faith of the reformers lies dormant. The giant sleeps in this city
and in the nation, oblivious to her world-shaking, world-changing
authority.

Against this background, our team composed of several churches
came together to pray for people in the city center. These sons and
daughters of the Scottish Reformation were unsure what to expect.
Few had witnessed the power of God on the streets. But as we set
out the chairs and then knelt to pray, the sense of faith grew. Perhaps
God would honor our faith, perhaps He would do what He alone
can do, and perhaps the kingdom would advance that day.

And then … nothing.

No sudden flood of people pouring forward for prayer. Nobody really noticed we were there. It wasn't long before the reality around us impacted the faith within us. But the kingdom advances through authority, not activity. We don't need to be busy to get breakthrough. So we waited.

Eventually, one lady came forward for prayer. She had broken a bone in her foot and was struggling to walk. A couple of team members began to pray. They took authority over the pain and commanded the bone to be repaired. Although the woman instantly felt relief, she wanted to walk around to confirm the improvement. After half an hour, she returned pain-free and completely healed. In St. Andrews, the city where the bones of martyrs were broken for the kingdom to advance, the bones of unbelievers were now restored as the church exercised spiritual authority.

And then … the floodgates opened.

The team prayed throughout the day, taking authority over all kinds of disease and sickness. It was wonderful to watch the church come alive. Some exercised their gift of evangelism, others served, while others still prayed. Joy was present. And hope was there too. One woman who had been deaf in one ear for a number of years took a seat. After the team prayed for about five minutes, she stood up, healed. St. Andrews, the city where the cry of the reformers had fallen on deaf ears, was now a place where the ears of the deaf were opened.

It was powerful. But as powerful as the healings were, the shift in mind-set of the team was even more wonderful. They suddenly "got it." They received a whole new vision of kingdom authority to supply the destiny of entire communities. And it happened on assignment!

Authority Grows on Assignment

You can't grow into authority any more than you can swim into a swimming pool. But you can grow in authority, which is given to us and grows as we give it to others. More accurately, it grows as we exercise it on behalf of others. The statement of Jesus "freely you have received, so freely give" is frequently used in the context of giving and receiving money, but originally it related to the giving and receiving of authority. Every time we spend our authority to serve others' destiny, authority grows in our lives. Every time we spend authority to bring life to the city, authority grows in our lives.

Authority multiplies when it is exercised. But it's not the only way we grow in authority.[18] Here are other ways:

Intimacy with God: We grow in authority when we grow in intimacy with God. While authority is not derived from intimacy, and can come without intimacy, authority increases with intimacy.[19] Proximity to Him means He immerses us with His name, His nature.

Submitting to governing authorities: We increase in authority when we recognize and submit to the structural and governing authorities in our nation. All authority is given by God. Responding with honor to public authority—as outlined in Romans 13—brings increased authority.

Humility: As we humble ourselves under God's mighty hand, reliant upon His intervention, He raises us up in due season.[20]

Handling adversity with maturity: In the kingdom, adversity is often a signpost to greater authority. Your rejection always contains your promotion. Jesus came out of the desert filled with the power of the Spirit.[21]

Generosity: What you do with your possessions determines your permission. Generosity is the gateway to greater authority. As you give it away, it increases. Whatever you keep is all you have, but whatever you give away God multiplies.

God desires that we increase in authority and that we release our authority to rewrite the story of the community.

Authority Changes the Atmosphere

Authority is given to change the atmosphere of cities, regions, and nations.

> Then Jesus came to them and said, "All authority in heaven and on earth has been given to me. Therefore go and make disciples of all nations, baptizing them in the name of the Father and of the Son and of the Holy Spirit, and teaching them to obey everything I have commanded you. And surely I am with you always, to the very end of the age."[22]

What we do with authority either grants or denies access for whole communities. Jesus phrased it this way: "I will give you the keys of the kingdom of heaven; whatever you bind on earth will be bound in heaven, and whatever you loose on earth will be loosed in heaven."[23] This is consistent with the pattern throughout Scripture where authority is given both to uproot and to plant. The prophet Jeremiah understood that his prophetic assignment involved both the building up and tearing down of nations.[24]

However, more recently, the church has focused more upon uprooting and demolishing demonic strongholds. Much prayer has been employed in the discerning and dismantling of demonic strongholds over cities and continents. While this is biblical and a legitimate use of kingdom authority, it is not the primary purpose of spiritual authority. The primary purpose of our authority is not to abolish the work of the enemy. Christ already accomplished this through the cross. The primary purpose of our authority is to *establish* a foundation that attracts the future. It is to create a place for the presence of God to fill. It is to prepare a people for the future that is coming.[25]

Spiritual authority used this way creates divine strongholds that alter the atmosphere of communities and cities—citadels of hope at the center of our cities. It allows us to speak to nations as catalysts of change.

Expect the church of the future to awaken to its creative, expansive authority. Expect it to manifest that authority in a way that opens possibilities for nations and generations. Expect it to erect citadels of hope in the midst of hurting humanity. Some of these citadels will be new churches that bring life, some will be compassion ministries that tackle injustice, some will be businesses that fuel opportunity, some will be artistic expressions, and some will be medical inventions that engender health for the soul and the body. Each of these divine strongholds is a planting of the Lord for the display of His splendor, and each of them changes the atmosphere of the city.

Chapter 11

BIGGER HEARTS FOR A BETTER CITY

Our rhythm was the same every Saturday night: at ten o'clock, our minibus full of food set out to search for rough sleepers in the city center. When we found them, we sat with them, served them food, and listened to their stories. And Eddie was a brilliant storyteller.

He was settling in for the night when we showed up. Huddled behind one of Glasgow's most famous buildings, Eddie had fashioned his own architectural masterpiece—cardboard boxes skillfully erected to protect his frail body from the elements. The pictures around him reflected his broken mind and emotions. Despite his history of broken relationships, Eddie was happy to see us. He always was. I'm not sure if our presence brought comfort, but at least it provided company.

Although the smell of urine filled the air, the fragrance of Jesus among us and especially with Eddie was unmistakable.

Later, as I arrived home reflecting on the evening, I felt the same emotions I often did after the "soup run" … thankful, guilty, frustrated. Thankful for the privilege of being with broken people and thankful God had been with us. Guilty that I was sleeping in a warm bed surrounded by people I loved. Frustrated that, although the poor had experienced relief, there was insufficient release. We had been good company for them but had not released destiny in them.

The Destiny of the Poor

I learned a valuable lesson through those experiences: the destiny of the poor is not the removal of poverty; the destiny of the poor is to rebuild broken cities.

This is the genius of the divine plan. God meets the discarded, destitute, and diseased, partnering with them to create new life in the city. The movement that transforms nations is started by the broken, not the brilliant. When God wants to awaken the city, He calls the people of compassion and restoration.

We find an example of this in the Old Testament. David's kingdom was birthed in a movement among the poor. The book of 1 Samuel tells us, "All those who were in distress or in debt or discontented gathered around him, and he became their commander. About four hundred men were with him."[1] These four hundred distressed and dismissed people would become the commanders of armies, engineers of cities, administrators of kingdoms, builders of communities, and restorers of places that had been ravaged by the enemy. As Isaiah prophesied in 61:1–4:

The Spirit of the Sovereign LORD is on me,
    because the LORD has anointed me
    to proclaim good news to the poor.
He has sent me to bind up the brokenhearted,
    to proclaim freedom for the captives
    and release from darkness for the prisoners,
to proclaim the year of the LORD's favor
    and the day of vengeance of our God,
to comfort all who mourn,
    and provide for those who grieve in Zion....
They will be called oaks of righteousness,
    a planting of the LORD
    for the display of his splendor.

They will rebuild the ancient ruins
    and restore the places long devastated;
they will renew the ruined cities
    that have been devastated for generations.

Notice the progression in the text. The Spirit moves among the poor (vv. 1–2). The poor become stronger (v. 3), and they release others (v. 4). The outcome of divine compassion is the renewal of cities that have suffered devastation for generations. And those who were previously devastated by loss are filled by God to restore the city. God doesn't just announce good news to the poor; He advances His kingdom through the poor. The poor are the people through whom God brings restoration. *They* will rebuild the ancient ruins, the places long devastated.

In the kingdom, compassion is not a gesture to the poor; it's a journey with the poor. This is where it was going all along ...

Not just God *helping* the poor.

Not just God *among* the poor.

Not just God *with* the poor.

But God *through* the poor making the community livable again.

The poor partner with God to "rebuild the ancient ruins ... restore the places long devastated ... renew the ruined cities ... devastated for generations."[2]

The Rescued Become the Rescuers

When I think of the poor partnering with God to restore places long devastated, I think of my mother. I was born on the south side of Glasgow, Scotland, into a family in the grip of brokenness. My father was slowly ending his brave battle with tuberculosis while my mum struggled to hold her young family and herself together. When Dad died, everything inside Mum broke, and so began a cycle of shame and pain in our family. Mum medicated her pain through alcohol and wrestled with addiction while my siblings and I simply fought for affection. It was all strangely normal in the community and the only life I ever knew. My earliest memories are marked not only by my father's absence but my mother's absence. Frequently her drinking would lead to nights in jail. Hers was a story of shame until Jesus rescued her.

The Bible says that those who have been forgiven much love much. And Mum did. She began to give away what had gripped her life. She made contact with local bakeries and agencies and, despite numerous setbacks and obstacles, developed our ministry to the poor known as the soup run. She traveled into the city center and spent time talking with and feeding the homeless. After a couple of nights, her vision broadened to include prostitutes. Each week she told me stories of new friends she had made, of God's grace in the moment.

As the soup run grew, other churches came to see it. Eventually they started their own ministry among the poor. Mum was delighted. Now there were more people bringing good news to the poor. One of her happiest nights was when her team arrived and there were two other "soup vans" present. It was clear churches were spurring one another on to love and good deeds. It was also clear to my mum that this phase of ministry was changing.

Over the next few months, she prayed about what area of ministry among the poor she should be involved in next. One day as she waited and prayed, she had a distinct vision of an African clergyman. Her sense was that this was a Holy Spirit prompting. She just didn't know what to do. Later that day, she attended prison fellowship, and when the speaker arrived she realized it was the man from her vision. He was an Anglican vicar from Malawi. As he spoke about the beauty of his country and the dreams of his community, my mother's heart broke again.

Not the brokenness of loss, but the brokenness of compassion, the brokenness of life disruption that comes when God births vision in a life.

She knew she had to facilitate the building of a mothers union. The mother who (by her own admission) had wrestled to raise her children now had vision for creating a center for mothers in Malawi. She built a relationship with Alex, the vicar, and later visited his country. It was the first time she had ever been outside the UK. When she returned home, she gathered people and poured vision into them. As they responded to the vision, they resourced the vision. Eventually a dilapidated building in a devastated region became a stronghold of education and hope for generations.

Mum wasn't just saved *from* something, she was saved *for* something. It's the destiny of the poor to bring life to nations.

Kingdom to the Margins

Jesus inaugurated a kingdom where formerly broken lives restore broken cities. He saw their misery, but He saw beyond their misery to their destiny. He knew their story of oppression *and* their journey of expansion. The poor were not His customers. The poor were His friends and fellow ministers. And so, the intentional movement of Jesus' life was toward the margins. It was toward the poor and the poor in spirit, the brokenhearted, the enslaved, the prisoners, the indebted, and the bereaved. His wasn't a moment of compassion; it was a movement of compassion.

Moved by compassion, Jesus taught: "And Jesus, when he came out, saw much people, and was moved with compassion toward them, because they were as sheep not having a shepherd: and he began to teach them many things."[3]

Moved by compassion, Jesus healed: "And Jesus, moved with compassion, put forth his hand, and touched him, and saith unto him, I will; be thou clean…. Jesus had compassion on them and touched their eyes. Immediately they received their sight and followed him."[4]

Moved by compassion, Jesus fed: "Jesus called his disciples to him and said, 'I have compassion for these people; they have already been with me three days and have nothing to eat. I do not want to send them away hungry, or they may collapse on the way.'"[5]

The movement of Jesus—whether it's healing, teaching, or feeding people—is a compassion movement, leading the poor into their purpose for living.

Power to Move the Poor toward Their Purpose

We need Holy Spirit power in order to move the poor toward their purpose. Without power, we can offer charity to the poor, but we cannot release their destiny. And charity is a poor substitute for destiny.

Imagine for a moment that Peter and John went off to pray. They met a lame man on the way. He asked them for alms and they gave them to him. And the man had some money that day. Charity without destiny. Now contrast it with the biblical narrative. Peter and John went off to pray. They met a lame man on the way who had been bypassed and had to beg his whole life. Filled with compassion, they spoke the words, "In the name of Jesus Christ of Nazareth, rise up and walk." Instantly the man's feet and ankles became strong. He rose up from dependency into destiny. He rose up beyond isolation into connection. He rose up from sickness to wholeness. Power brought wholeness to the whole man.

Supernatural ministry demonstrates to the poor that there is a power at work on their behalf capable of transforming individuals and redeeming communities. The powers that oppress the poor must be overthrown by a power at work on behalf of the poor. Since the love of power oppresses the poor, only the power of love releases the oppressed. It is not enough to emulate the heart of Jesus; we must demonstrate the power of Jesus. In Luke 4:18–19, Jesus read from the book of Isaiah in the synagogue, saying:

> The Spirit of the Lord is on me,
>> because he has anointed me
>> to proclaim good news to the poor.
> He has sent me to proclaim freedom for the
>> prisoners
>> and recovery of sight for the blind,
> to set the oppressed free,
>> to proclaim the year of the Lord's favor.

The Spirit of the Sovereign Lord is upon me to bring good news to the poor. Without the empowering presence of the Holy Spirit, there is no good news for the poor.

Compassion and Mission Are Inseparable

Some are nervous around spiritual power, and with good reason. We certainly don't need more people embarking on the Great Commission without great compassion.[6]

I have witnessed exercise of spiritual power without compassion. It bothers me. Approaching strangers to increase our boldness rather than release captives is always wrong. Anything not rooted in love is devoid of true power. The excesses of exercising spiritual power without compassion are well documented and the stories often told. It never ends well. Power without compassion destroys those who wield it.

However, it should equally trouble us when believers claim acts of mercy while ignoring spiritual power. Just as healthy community is more than social networking, compassion is more than social enterprises. It is greater than social activism.[7] Compassion has its origins in the heart of God and is rooted in the nature, character, and order of God. It is inherently and intrinsically supernatural.

It is not enough to have social concern; we must have the Spirit with power. Justice and supernatural power are connected.[8] The church is designed to be a healing community, and we can no longer separate what God has joined together. Works of mercy and works of power belong together. We are the people of miracles *and* mercy. Those of us who love miracles are being called to love mercy too.[9] Those of us who love mercy are called to walk in the miraculous. It's the Jesus way.

The Spirit of Mission Is the Spirit of Mercy

Jesus refused to send His followers to care for bruised lives without power.

"Jesus called twelve of his followers and sent them into the ripe fields. He gave them power to kick out the evil spirits and to tenderly care for the bruised and hurt lives."[10]

This fits the biblical pattern: the spirit of mission is the spirit of might and the spirit of mercy. We cannot divorce mercy from mission or carry out our mission without power. There are already too many disillusioned believers who initiated acts of mercy without having sufficient power to release the oppressed.

I'm reminded of Mo, who grew up surrounded by wealth and opulence. He had several servants who ensured his every desire was fulfilled. His societal status gave him affluence, influence, and more than a little arrogance. And then the justice awakening happened in him. He realized that everything he owned had been built through oppression. It was more than he could stomach, so he took action. Violent action.

On the surface, his actions seemed governed by compassion. He removed the instrument of Egyptian oppression using the strength he had. He assumed those around him would be inspired by his activism and lend their support. However, the wider community failed to recognize or respond to the hope he was offering. His early efforts to bring an end to injustice and bring life to the broken led to fatigue and brokenness in his own soul.

Broken and disappointed by the experience, Mo retreated from the city to the wilderness. About as far from people as he could. He had acted to help the marginalized. And then he was numbered among them with no strength, no solution, and little concern.

> Now Moses was tending the flock of Jethro his father-in-law, the priest of Midian, and he led the flock to the far side of the wilderness and came to Horeb, the mountain of God. There the angel of the LORD appeared to him in flames of fire from within a bush. Moses saw that though the bush was on fire it did not burn up. So Moses thought, "I will go over and see this strange sight—why the bush does not burn up."

When the LORD saw that he had gone over to look, God called to him from within the bush, "Moses! Moses!"

And Moses said, "Here I am."

"Do not come any closer," God said. "Take off your sandals, for the place where you are standing is holy ground." Then he said, "I am the God of your father, the God of Abraham, the God of Isaac and the God of Jacob." At this, Moses hid his face, because he was afraid to look at God.

The LORD said, "I have indeed seen the misery of my people in Egypt. I have heard them crying out because of their slave drivers, and I am concerned about their suffering. So I have come down to rescue them from the hand of the Egyptians and to bring them up out of that land into a good and spacious land, a land flowing with milk and honey—the home of the Canaanites, Hittites, Amorites, Perizzites, Hivites and Jebusites. And now the cry of the Israelites has reached me, and I have seen the way the Egyptians are oppressing them. So now, go. I am sending you to Pharaoh to bring my people the Israelites out of Egypt."[11]

God visits the burned-out activist and reminds him that He is concerned for people. In that place, God restored Moses' calling to engage with suffering humanity, but this time to do so with the power of love. This time he wouldn't operate from his own anger, his own strength. This time there would be signs and wonders that accompanied the message of deliverance and expansive hope. In this way, prevailing love would conquer injustice.

Beyond Raising Awareness

Moses already knew it would take more than human compassion to move these people from the margins. So he asked,

> "What if they do not believe me or listen to me and say, 'The LORD did not appear to you'?"
>
> Then the LORD said to him, "What is that in your hand?"
>
> "A staff," he replied.
>
> The LORD said, "Throw it on the ground."
>
> Moses threw it on the ground and it became a snake, and he ran from it. Then the LORD said to him, "Reach out your hand and take it by the tail." So Moses reached out and took hold of the snake and it turned back into a staff in his hand. "This," said the LORD, "is so that they may believe that the LORD, the God of their fathers—the God of Abraham, the God of Isaac and the God of Jacob— has appeared to you."[12]

Moses' fresh encounter gave him power to move beyond raising awareness.[13] Raising awareness is good, but it's not what Jesus called us to do. He anointed us to release captives. The purpose of compassion is not empathy; the purpose of compassion is transformation. Such transformation is only possible and sustainable through the dynamic empowering of God. Power is given so that we can live lives of supernatural compassion, so that we can live lives of *sustainable* compassion.

This is the lesson Moses learns. We can move to the margins in our own strength and end up burned out, buried under others' approval or disapproval, or we can receive power that helps the marginalized experience community.

Living without compassion isn't an option.

Neither is going without power.

Thankfully, we don't have to choose between the supernatural and social justice. We don't have to choose between miracles and mercy. Compassion pulls us from the corners of our preference and leads us to the corners of the earth.

Recently our church felt powerless and numb as we watched scenes of Syrian refugees fleeing for their lives. Compassion demanded action. But the sheer scale of the crisis seemed beyond us. We did what we could in our gathered environments, leveraging the potential of the pulpit to inspire people toward local action. We encouraged each member to speak to their employer about ways their company could take action. One person worked at the Bushmills whisky distillery and her boss agreed to host a breakfast, donating the proceeds. Others did similar things. As a church we raised an offering and prayed for agencies involved at the forefront of relief efforts. Yet we knew it was insufficient. Our compassion still fit in the building. It had moved us, but it hadn't messed us up. We were emotional but not empowered.

So we moved to the next level and engaged in structured compassion. We sent a team to a refugee camp primarily to assess needs and identify ways we could make a greater contribution. When they arrived, they were overwhelmed. It was difficult to know where to start or what to do. So they did what they always do. They began praying for the sick. And as they did, many were healed, with the result that people came to them from all over the camp. It wasn't everything they hoped, but it was a starting point.

The next time, they went out on their own. It wasn't structured compassion; it was spontaneous. When they arrived, they discovered the government planned to close the camp and forcibly evict the refugees. One of the team members, deeply disturbed, turned her distress into inspiration to create a solution. She used her skills in writing proposals to draft a document requesting that the refugees each receive vitamins.

When the team returned to the camps, this is what happened:

> On our third day, we went to a huge camp, and many of the people living there were hopeless and depressed. The heat was intense. We met a family with whom we had spent time in Idomeni. There was a lot of tears and laughter. Many refugees gathered around us to see what all the excitement was about. A man called Mohammed came up to one of us and asked a lot of questions about who we were and what we were doing. He asked about our God and said he had the only true faith in Allah.

Later on that afternoon, two of us were giving out vitamins, going from tent to tent, when Mohammed approached. He asked us to come with him to see a lady. Her son had been stabbed the night before and was now quite sick. When we went to the tent, the mother was very upset. She said her son was losing a lot of blood and was at the sink area in the camp trying to stop the bleeding. Although I wasn't allowed to act as a doctor in the camps, I told Mohammed that if he could find the man, I would have a look at his wounds.

Meanwhile two other members of the team were distributing vitamins in another part of the camp and they found the young man who had been stabbed. They offered to pray for his stab wounds and he said yes. Just then, Mohammed arrived. He watched as Diane prayed for the man. The bleeding stopped and he was able to get up. The color returned to his face and his wounds closed over. People started to dance and we walked with the young man back to his mother's tent. She was amazed and delighted to see that he had been healed.

Just after that, Mohammed found two other team members and said, "Don't worry about the young man who has been stabbed. Your friends found him and prayed with him. Your Jesus has healed him."

"God anointed Jesus of Nazareth with the Holy Spirit and power, and how he went around doing good and healing all who were under the power of the devil, because God was with him."[14]

Compassion in the Hands of Scattered Servants

Scattered servants go around doing good, releasing compassion, and healing because God is with them.

They are not pursuing their own cause; they are following Christ. So they move beyond the building, not due to disillusionment or discontentment with church, but because they have been envisioned by the story God is inscribing on all of humanity. As a result, they can no longer live in the narrowness of Sunday services alone, or simply sponsoring the good works of other agencies. It's not enough for them to minister out of programs; they must minister out of the presence. They are *moved* by the Spirit of God to live out their influence in a way that makes a difference among the least, the lowest, and the lost.

The kingdom, in the hands of these scattered servants, goes beyond meetings. It goes beyond ministry, into the heart of broken humanity.

Greg wanted to create a vegetable garden on our site and use the produce to feed the poor. The only problem was that our site was concrete. There was nowhere to plant a garden. Undeterred, Greg suggested we use tractor tires as a base for planting seeds. It seemed unusual to me, not to mention unsightly. We had recently moved into our purpose-built facility, and after years of renting, we were keen to create a good impression. Tractor tires visible to guests didn't seem like the way forward. But it had compassion at the core, so we agreed to Greg's vision.

One day while we were giving a tour to some local government officials, they noticed the tires and asked what we were doing. Greg and Ricky, our Compassion director, explained the broad vision. We intended to grow vegetables and use them to feed people. Greg and Ricky outlined our vision to grow this ministry until we had an allotment where unemployed folks and those suffering with depression could participate in helping things grow. Much to their surprise, the officials said, "We would love to give you £10,000 toward this idea."

So we bought a polytunnel, erected it in a corner of our site, and upgraded our vegetable garden. There were more space and more produce, and people came from everywhere to help. The reduction of alienation and sense of community were clear. People were growing produce and finding purpose. Still we knew there were others in the community who perhaps weren't interested in horticulture but loved to make things. So Martin, a former alcoholic turned business owner, suggested we use part of our site to create a woodshop. And so we converted one of our old timber sheds into a log-producing warehouse.

Some of the first people to come were former police officers suffering with post-traumatic stress disorder. The rhythm of the work seemed to calm them. Plus there was always an end product. It got done. After years of encountering problems that never seemed to be fixed, the logs were fixed. It was therapy and community. There were others who came. One of the local prisons asked us to consider working with prisoners on day release. Each week a busload came from the prison, and the prisoners spent the day in community. And so the police officers and prisoners worked together for the sake of others.

After a while the governor of the prison called us. He wanted to know about a prisoner who had been working with our team. The prisoner was notorious for being an obstructionist. He filed daily complaints, and although he never won a single one, he gained great satisfaction from knowing each one had to be investigated. His antics made the lives of the senior officers more difficult. The governor told us that from the day he started working in the log warehouse, he hadn't filed one complaint. Then he asked, "How do I create that in my prison? And would you be willing to help train our officers to do it?"

Only God can revive stories and reclaim lives. Only generous compassion can make it happen.

A Culture of Generous Compassion

Generous compassion is the culture of heaven. It is the sign that we are carrying the life of God, the indicator His life is changing our lives. The Lord is gracious and compassionate, and He rises to show us compassion. As He breathes His life into us, we build bigger hearts for a better city. We live and love beyond ourselves. Although compassion may *start* in church, it never *stays* in church. Compassion is too big to fit in the building. It is too great to be confined to a program.

We discovered this again recently as we hosted a formal for one of our local schools. It is a wonderful school with exceptional children. Each of the kids is placed in the school because they have particular needs that require assistance and attention. The children are among the most loving you could ever hope to meet.

Throughout the history of the school, there had never been sufficient resources to hold a formal. When we heard this, we sensed the invitation of the Father to partner with Him and the school in creating the first-ever formal. During the planning phase of the event, we included the kids, welcoming their imagination and input for the event. Naturally, we also made our church community aware of what we intended to do.

As you can imagine, the response from our church was overwhelming. What was even greater was the response of our city. The Father's dreams are big, and beyond the church they always intersect with the city. One large department store in a nearby city heard what we were doing and provided racks of formal dresses for the girls to choose from. It was simply beautiful.

A leading photographer in the nation heard about it and offered his time, free of charge, so the kids and parents could have quality photos and treasured memories. One gentleman offered the services of his limousine company, followed by another company, to help the kids feel special. On the two Saturdays before the formal, the girls arrived with their parents to choose their dresses. It was like watching several brides choose their wedding dresses all at once.

And then things started shifting in the atmosphere of the school. Our kids' pastor emailed me the following:

> Just wanted to let you in on what's happening down
> at the school. I felt the Lord wanted to do significant

healing with the young people at the school on the evening of the formal. I felt that as they experienced His kingdom, some of their physical and mental conditions would change. However, according to reports from the school, change is already happening. Parents are reporting that one young person who rocks back and forth continually has stopped and is now calm. Another, who is subject to fits of aggression, is now at peace. Another who previously spent the days groaning and moaning now sings. Parents have been given hope that there is acceptance and love for their children—with no strings attached and from a church! One of the teachers said that last week she was approached on four separate occasions by students—three asking questions about Jesus and one asking for a Bible. This has never happened before.

We were beginning to wonder just how special the night would be.

On the night itself, the girls arrived, as did the boys. Everyone was wearing their formal attire—and wearing wide smiles. Proud parents stood on the steps leading into the church, watching the limousines pull up. And then the moment when their child stepped out and were seen. Seen as they had always seen them. Seen in all their beauty. Faces moved from smiling to crying in moments … and then the rapturous applause as the guard of honor formed.

Inside the venue, each child was greeted and given a drink before taking a seat in the car we had brought in especially for the occasion. Their excitement was contagious and their joy infectious.

After some mingling, the meal was served. During the meal, prizes were given to each child. It was unlike any celebration or prize day I had ever attended. Every kid cheered for the others, not politely but raucously as though they themselves had been awarded the prize. There was no polite, quiet acceptance of the prizes either—full emotion was on display. And although the prizes were small, the joy at receiving them was huge.

After the meal it was time to have their photographs taken. Some hair was licked, some bow ties were straightened, and then the clicking began. And then the dance. I had been a little nervous beforehand as some kids' needs were severe and they were wheelchair-bound. I needn't have worried. The moment the music started, every kid piled onto the dance floor. It was unrestrained and beautiful. And by the end of the night there were parents and children and grandfathers and volunteers on the floor together.

It was an incredible night, and it all started with a God-idea in the heart of a scattered servant.

When compassion grips our lives, it enlarges our lives. We build bigger hearts for better cities.

Chapter 12

REVIVAL TOWN

It's the task of the church to rewrite the story of the city.

A couple of our staff participated in a leadership conference in South Africa. Their mission was to share various ways the church could increase effectiveness beyond the building. After the session they did something different. They invited delegates to come with them to the community of Colesberg.

Like many communities, Colesberg had a reputation for resistance to the gospel. Prevailing wisdom stated it was a "difficult-to-reach" area. Ironically, the town was founded on an abandoned station of the London Missionary Society.[1] But now, indicators suggested a widespread disinterest in the kingdom of God. Undeterred, the team showed up in central Colesberg and invited anyone whose life was broken to receive prayer. They prayed for the sick for hours, witnessing multiple healings and several people coming to faith.

Unknown to them, they were being watched.

Two policemen who had been monitoring their movements came to them with an unusual request. "There is a school in our area where some of the kids are engaging in occultic practice. We don't have power to stop them, but we can see that you do. Would you be willing to come to the school?" Well, what do you say when the police ask you to accompany them? It's not wise to refuse. So after thinking for a moment, the team answered with an emphatic yes and set out for the school.

When they arrived at the school, the children had already been gathered from their classes and were assembled in one place. Unsure what to do next, the team asked if anyone would like prayer. Four hundred hands shot in the air! Since it was too many to pray for individually, the team prayed their best prayer over the whole group. When they had finished praying, the police officers had another request. "Would you mind coming with us to the police station?" Once again, what do you say when the police ask you to accompany them? You can hardly say no! So the policemen took them to the station, where they prayed for every officer, including the chief of police.

And the rumor now is that Colesberg is not so difficult to reach after all. It's just really hard to reach when the church stays in the building.

Reaching Our Towns and Cities

Jesus had passion for reaching towns and cities. "News about him spread quickly over the whole region of Galilee."[2] As a result, people began hearing an alternative story. A story of hope and healing supplanted the prevailing narrative and filled the region. Hope had come to town. The name of Jesus was on the lips of everyone throughout the region as His kingdom story inscribed fresh hope into weary communities. Things were changing, gathering momentum.

Once a new story starts, it spreads quickly. It wasn't long before "the whole town gathered at the door."[3]

Picture the scene: a whole community *alive* with kingdom expectation. The shift in the spiritual climate over an entire town caused everyone to draw near to what God was doing in their midst. Everyone longing to gain a glimpse of Jesus, everyone pressing into the kingdom story. Until recently they had been or seemed disinterested, disconnected, disempowered. Now the power of God was breaking out, bodies and stories were changed, all of it fueling hunger and intangible hope. Suddenly, everywhere you looked in town people were looking for God. Not secretly or subtly, but tangibly and visibly. The community could no longer curtail or control their hunger. They must have more of the life of God.

"[Jesus,] everyone is looking for you!"[4]

It's the dream of every pastor to have people queuing up outside the doors of the church longing to witness the inbreaking of the kingdom of God. Sometimes the dream becomes reality.

In 1859, our whole town was filled with the presence of God and people were drawn from miles around. People without interest in God were suddenly captivated by Him, and people who had lived without God could do so no longer. Those who would not go near a church were falling under the power of the Holy Spirit on the streets and had to be carried into churches for shelter. Everything and everyone was under a different climate.

199

The atmosphere was charged with divine favor. Everyone was looking for God. What happened in one person spilled over onto others, until it spilled into the whole region. Revival historian J. Edwin Orr described it this way:

> Coleraine was favoured with special visitations of power and blessing. In one of the schools a boy came under conviction so much that the teacher sent him home with an older boy who had been converted only the previous day. On the way home they turned into an empty house to pray together. The troubled boy was soon rejoicing and said, "I must go back and tell the teacher." With a beaming face he told him, "O sir I am so happy I have the Lord Jesus in my heart."
>
> The whole class was affected as a result and boy after boy rose and silently left the room. When the teacher went to investigate he found them ranged around the playground wall on their knees. Silent prayer soon gave way to loud cries and prayers, which carried to the girls' school on the first floor. Immediately the girls fell on their knees and wept. The commotion carried into the street; neighbors and passers-by came flocking in. As soon as they crossed the threshold, they all came under the same convicting power.
>
> Ministers came to help, men of prayer were summoned, and the day was spent in leading young

and old to saving faith in Christ. On June 7th a great open-air meeting was held in Coleraine where converts testified. Such large crowds gathered that they were divided into several groups, each to be addressed by different ministers. God's presence was an awesome reality. Many came under deep conviction. Many prostrations occurred.

It continued throughout the following day and in the evening the market was crowded. The gospel was preached and again many sank down and with bitter cries sought the Lord for mercy. Christian helpers took many of these "stricken ones" as they were now called into the new town hall, then awaiting its official opening. A Bible is still there with this inscription, "It is meant to be a memorial of the first opening of the new town hall when upon the night of June 9th, nearly one hundred persons agonised in mind through conviction of sin, and entirely prostrate in body, were brought into that building to obtain shelter during the night, and to receive consolation from the instructions and prayers of Christian ministers and Christian people."[5]

We started church planting in our community with the echoes of those stories stirring our souls. Kingdom expectation gripped our hearts. We were filled with anticipation that once again divine favor would cover our area, causing everyone to look and long for the living God. Our history told us that it was not madness to believe such things could happen.

It is possible. "Jesus, everyone is looking for you!"

Hope-Filled Eyes

While everyone was looking for Him, Jesus was looking beyond …

> Beyond addition to multiplication.
> Beyond the moment to the movement.
> Beyond gathering to scattering.
> Beyond *some* hearing and responding, to *everyone*
> hearing and responding.

So Jesus replied, "Let us go somewhere else—to the nearby villages—so I can preach there also. That is why I have come."[6]

Jesus came to bring back life to *every* city. It wasn't enough for Him to have larger, ever-increasing gatherings. He wanted more than a greater number of conversions, even more than a great awakening in His hometown. His desire was nothing less than the whole earth— every community, all of humanity—filled and fueled with the glory of God. He believed it was possible, perhaps even inevitable. As a result, He saw every community with hope-filled eyes.

Even communities that the church had written off were written into His heart. Communities like Sychar in Samaria were vulnerable to hope, subject to change. So as Jesus sat at a well in town, He said to His disciples, "Don't you have a saying, 'It's still four months until harvest'? I tell you, open your eyes and look at the fields! They are ripe for harvest."[7]

In effect Jesus says, "You think a move of God is far off, but I tell you it is accelerating." In this town at this time: in your town at this time.

"Even now the one who reaps draws a wage and harvests a crop for eternal life, so that the sower and the reaper may be glad together."[8]

As Jesus spoke, something moved. Some*one* moved.

The Samaritan woman began sharing her story with her community. Her story created a shift. People were drawn—disrupted from their normal daily rhythm—and moved to apprehend the grace of God. Her story reset the spiritual climate in a town the disciples had just visited. They showed up as tourists. She showed up as a transformed woman. She who was known as a loose woman was now loosing revival.

Her story is a prophetic picture of what happens when every believer walks in divine favor. Sadly, we keep *waiting* on the harvest instead of *carrying* the harvest. Somehow, we think it hard to change the reputation of one woman in our town, while Jesus declares that now is the time for the story of the whole town to be rewritten.

I believe these are days when what had been reserved is being released, days when we experience favor where we have not labored. While parts of the body of Christ focus upon an "end-time harvest," God waits to give us a renewed-mind harvest. We search for the kingdom in the dramatic, all the while missing the dynamic small moments that change one destiny and reset the trajectory of an entire city.

There was an atmospheric shift in the city as the whole community came under the influence of one woman's story of hope. Although spiritual receptivity marked the climate of the city, the disciples missed the whole thing. Staggering. Excusable if Jesus hadn't trained these men for years to discern and enter the kingdom. Understandable if they had no framework or history in reaching towns and cities. But they had taken ministry trips together where whole towns were awakened to the kingdom. They *knew* it was possible. Yet every one of them missed the move of God beyond their border. No one had faith for Samaria. Since they hadn't sown in that area, they had no expectation of reaping.

So Jesus reminds them: "I sent you to reap what you have not worked for. Others have done the hard work, and you have reaped the benefits of their labor."[9]

With these words He reframes their perspective of what is possible—of what is available in every community as scattered servants show up. If God can do it in Samaria, He can do it in any area. He can do it in your area. He can do it in mine. Passages like this one are designed to hook our hearts, to fuel our hunger, to awaken us to the adventure of favor gripping whole regions. They are not primarily for small-group Bible study but for whole-community transformation. The works of God are eternal. Always available. Always accessible.

Coleraine—Shifting into Our Inheritance

We carry a belief and growing conviction that whole towns, even regions, will turn to Jesus when they hear about all He is doing.

When they heard about all he was doing, many
people came to him from Judea, Jerusalem, Idumea,
and the regions across the Jordan and around Tyre
and Sidon.[10]

And toward the end of 2013, we experienced the first sudden
shift.

It started in October.

That month was unusual because so many people were pressing
into the kingdom in all of our environments. While it was common
to see thirty or forty folks come to faith each month, during that
October there were over ninety new believers. We were excited by
their stories and intrigued by the bigger story of God. We knew it
was a sign. We didn't know what it was pointing us toward.

Thankfully we had scheduled a couple of prophetic voices to
address our community during the month of November. The first
one to speak referenced what was happening among us. He said,
"This month you have seen on average three people a day come to
faith. It has astounded you, but I tell you that from this day you are
going to see between five and ten people a day coming to faith."

It sounded bold.

It sounded beyond us.

Yet we believed.

The following week, thirty-five people came to faith. Exactly
five a day! We were excited by what was happening in the hearts of
individuals. We were also intrigued by what it might mean for the
future of our community. We had leaned into stewardship over the
previous years, so we knew that when God releases something it is

supposed to stay present. We were also aware that we had entered new territory, and what once seemed exceptional (ninety people coming to faith in a month) was really the new normal. God was raising the temperature in our area and raising the bar of our faith.

But not before another story presented itself to our hearts. On the last day of the week, the shadow story emerged. A young man with whom we had worked over the years (witnessing occasional moments of tangible hope) had received a beating. Not your average everyday beating, but a "punishment beating." He had been shot in front of his family in his own home. This was exactly the opposite to the script we had been handed by the Father just days earlier.

We weren't witnessing *revival* of young people in our community; we were witnessing *removal* of young people from our community. It vied for the attention of our hearts, and we refused to bow to its voice. Instead we leaned in more intentionally to what we knew our Father had spoken. He had given us a glimpse of what *He* had for us. It was now our task to contend and pursue in order for that initial breakthrough to be established among us. So we kept pressing in while processing pain. We positioned ourselves for what we believed God was leading us into, despite how things appeared.

We had an inkling things were shifting, and we wanted to move some people onto the streets more permanently. At the beginning of 2014, we identified and appointed evangelists. We commissioned them in faith, believing God would use them to lead many to faith.

Truthfully, none of us really expected what happened next. It seemed as if all heaven broke loose.

We discovered the atmosphere in our town really had changed. We were now in a very different climate—a spiritually responsive and receptive climate. People began showing up at church because God had spoken to them in dreams. Unbelievers began driving to our car park simply to be healed. Whole families were encountering the love of God. It was happening in our gathered environments and it was happening on our streets.

Our evangelists were praying for many and initially seeing lots of healing and a few people coming to faith.

In March 2014, one of them asked his daughter one morning, "How many people are going to become Christians today?" At that time our teams were seeing maybe four or five people come to faith in a day, so for us the idea that we would see more than that in a day just was inconceivable. This man's daughter looked at him and said, "You're going to see ten come to faith today, Daddy." And she was referring to just his evangelistic work, no one else's. And he thought, *Oh no, I'm not going to see ten. She's going to be disappointed.* He began to worry he had raised her hopes and she would be greatly disappointed.

At lunchtime he met with his wife, who was aware of the conversation with his daughter. "Three people have come to faith," he reported. At about three thirty in the afternoon, he thought, *What am I going to tell my girl?* He looked across the street and saw a group of seven lads. Quick calculations confirmed that these seven plus the previous three would equal the ten he was looking for. He walked over to them and delivered this opening line: "God told me I was going to see ten people come to faith in Him today. I've seen three, and you're my other seven." And it was true. Every one of them gave their life to Jesus. The evangelist went home happy.

In those days it seemed harder for people *not* to come to faith than to come to faith. It didn't seem to matter whether they were from the town or a tourist.

In July 2014, a Spanish lady, a French lady, and a German lady visited our town, and a couple of guys on our team engaged the three women in conversation on the streets. One of the ladies was an atheist and the other two were ambivalent. They hadn't set out that day to look for God, but God was looking for them. As the guys began talking to them, the atheist lady began to withdraw from the conversation and the other two remained. They spoke a little bit more, listened to what was said, and within ten minutes gave their lives to Jesus. And that would be a stunning story if that's where it ended—but sitting on a nearby seat was a sixty-nine-year-old man with his wife who overheard the whole thing. He approached the guys with a beaming smile on his face and said, "I want to know this Jesus." And right then he gave his life to Jesus—along with his wife.

Such events happened so frequently that nothing seemed impossible. One of our church members, James, had bought a new dog. As a result, he joined an army of inexperienced dog walkers. He discovered a community of disciplined people who walk their dogs in the same place at the same time every day. Ever alert to kingdom moments, James imagined what it would look like for the kingdom to show up in the woods. On one occasion, he noticed a man who regularly jogged with his dog, but today was reduced to walking. James approached him and asked if he was in pain. The man said he was, and so James offered to pray for the pain to leave. When the man was healed, James invited him to faith, and there and then he gave his life to Jesus.

And so it was that the kingdom of God came crashing into the world of dogs. It's a remarkable story. Made all the more so because James has since led eight others to faith in the woods with their dogs.

One eleven-year-old girl woke earlier than usual on a Saturday morning. But she woke with a plan. Her intention was to recruit a friend and then head into town. She immediately set to work texting her friend. They met together in the town center and embarked upon the task of leading people to Jesus. By the time they returned home that afternoon, over twenty people had come to faith for the first time. It didn't once enter their heads that the mission would be difficult or fruitless.

Beyond Revival to Rewriting the Story

For the next couple of years, we felt like we were living in revival town. On the outside it looked like a sudden move of God. On the inside it looked like a gradual move of His people. On the outside it looked utterly sovereign. On the inside it looked like partnership. In truth, God was doing something we could never do. He was doing it through scattered servants on the streets of our town, and it changed the story of our community and created an even greater atmospheric shift over our area.

We love revival. Yet because we have been here before as a community and witnessed unprecedented numbers of people show interest in the kingdom, we know that we need something more than a sudden move of God. We want something that is sustainable across generations, something that can be stewarded by our children's children. We want to become a reformation town.

As for us, our mind-set has moved from seeing our community resistant, to seeing it as receptive, to seeing revival outpourings, and now we are pressing in to reformation. Rewriting the story of our city so that it increasingly comes under the influence of the Lord Jesus Christ in every environment. We want there to be the tangible, unmistakable fragrance of His presence filling everything in our city. We want our city to become a resting place for His glory.

The days are coming when whole regions will come alive. There's an increase of power coming; it's more than we have had before; it's more than we have seen before. It's a new normal. It's an acceleration of favor. It is a fresh favor on us for a new future for our streets, for our cities.

Chapter 13

LOVING OUR CITIES INTO LIFE

It was a phrase I had heard before and even used a few times myself. Today it seemed more satisfying pouring from the lips of a young church planter we sent from our church two years previously. "We don't really have a vision for our church; we have a dream for our city." Andy proceeded to share stories of partnership with the police, working in local communities, of starting ministries only where programs and external agencies didn't exist already.

As his stories filled and ignited the room, it reminded me we almost missed the adventure of bringing life to the city. We *almost* settled for building a better church, almost reduced our vision of the kingdom to what we thought was possible and available.

While our journey toward the city has been intentional, it didn't start that way. Initially we were just trying to gather enough people from our city so we could build a church. We accidentally discovered

God's heart for the city. Incrementally the largeness of God leaned into the life of our church, and we experienced His affection for our community.

It has always been God's intention to restore beauty and bring life to all things through His church. The apostle Paul said, "And God placed all things under his feet and appointed him to be head over everything for the church, which is his body, the fullness of him who fills everything in every way."[1]

Scriptures like this awakened our imagination and invited us to dream of a different city. Initially the dreams were stored in our hearts. Eventually we shared them with others, finding confidence to wonder aloud.

What if the kingdom *is* big enough for the whole city?

What if God's intention is for the church to fill *all* things?

What if we were known as the dreamers over the city?

What if we became partners with the city?

What if together we rewrote the story of the city, filling it with generous glory?

We began to realize it was possible. But to see it happen, we were going to have to start thinking differently.

The Possibility of Leading Cities into Life

Jesus sent His disciples with a mandate to bring life to broken cities. "After this the Lord appointed seventy-two others and sent them two by two ahead of him to every town and place where he was about to go."[2]

Notice, He sent His disciples to cities in line for a divine visitation, every place He was about to go. He also sent them with the expectation that city formation was possible.

While Jesus believed that cities, even nations, would be responsive to the kingdom, much of modern discipleship has focused upon making believers strong enough to survive the city rather than bold enough to transform the city. We have excelled in creating disciples, just not the kind that change cities or shift societies. Our churches grow larger while our cities grow darker.

The expectation of city formation has been reduced and replaced with an emphasis upon spiritual formation. City formation is deemed unattainable, so we look for something more doable, more manageable—the perfection of an individual rather than the alteration of a city. As a result, we have practiced great reduction with the Great Commission. We have beautifully and relentlessly focused on the salvation or transformation of individuals but missed the kingdom invitation that facilitates the alteration of institutions, even whole cities.

The problem with this method is that it engenders a mind-set of introspection rather than expansion. From the outset we introduce the thought that it is difficult to reach the city, a thought alien to the mind of Christ. It never once entered Jesus' mind that His disciples would have difficulty discipling nations, let alone cities. Yet we have taken His commission and considered it impossible. This worldview is a betrayal of the generosity of God and the victory of Christ. He is enough for our families and our cities.

His kingdom is big enough for the whole city.

The Kingdom Is Big Enough for Every City

The largest city in the UK is the beautiful London. There is nowhere quite like it for history, pageantry, and destiny. Yet London also has proliferated brokenness raging under the surface of its streets. The prevalence of violence, consumerism, and indifference to faith has convinced many that London is becoming increasingly secularized with more and more people disinterested in Christ.

It's a familiar story, a fascinating story. It's just not true.

It fails to account for the pervasive prevailing kingdom in the hands of scattered servants. The whole kingdom in the hands of scattered servants is enough for any city. It is enough for every city. Even London.

We discovered this when we sent a team to serve at the London Olympics in the summer of 2012. Their responsibility was to train people to pray for the sick on the streets around various Olympic venues. Our members are convinced that no city is beyond reach, so they saw what they expected to see: people queuing to be prayed for in public. Englishmen and women risked reputation to enter the kingdom. The sociological and cultural arguments that insisted London was different, or indifferent, gave way to the greater reality that people everywhere are desperately hurting and secretly hoping. As the team prayed, they witnessed many moments of intervention with numbers of people being healed from minor ailments to major conditions.

As they continued praying, a young man took to the seats. One of the team members sensed he was estranged from his father and involved in gang culture. As they shared this information, the young man poured out his story. He told them that due to his involvement in recent violence, he was on the run from rival gangs. In fact, at that moment he was carrying a gun. He didn't know he was making that confession to someone responsible for training police officers. He didn't know he was repenting because the kingdom was near. He didn't have that theology. All he knew was that he wanted to get right with God. So he did.

Later, as the day closed, the team huddled together to share their stories of favor and failure. As they did, they were interrupted by a bystander who had been listening to their accounts of healing. With tears running down the man's face, he called out, "Yes, but how can my sins be forgiven?"

It's possible to reach our cities, but there is no easy or quick-fix solution for the pain in our cities.

Every city has problems. Every city knows the struggle of pain and shame, of addiction and relational dysfunction. Every city has a shadow story that masquerades as "normal" and creates a sense of hopelessness. But change is indeed possible.

Just look at the ancient city of Nineveh. It was a "sin city" renowned for oppression, corruption, and idolatrous devotion. It had a reputation for violence and brutality. Its shadow story was strong, loud, and frightening. Yet it was to Nineveh the scattered servant Jonah was sent.

Yes, *that* Jonah.

In this familiar story, the focus is usually on Jonah's miraculous encounter with a fish. But the primary focus, the real story, is about Jonah's miraculous repentance and restoration of an entire city. *That* is what set it apart. It was a new kind of story, a new scale of redemption—the revelation of God's great love for broken cities everywhere. It was the first invitation for God's children to step into a new kind of divine partnership, one that could rewrite the story of the whole community beyond the walls of the church.

And it almost didn't happen.

As the story opens, Jonah is more intent on protecting his righteousness than bringing life to the city. Jonah was more aware of the reputation of the city than the reality of the kingdom. He was more concerned with making his point than releasing hope.

It doesn't take a prophet to condemn the city. But it takes a prophet to co-labor with God until life comes to the city.

It doesn't take a prophet to see the reputation of a city. But it takes a prophet to see the restoration of a city.

It doesn't take a prophet to outline the failure of the city. But it takes a prophet to highlight the favor on a city.

It doesn't take a prophet to write off the city. But it takes a prophet to rewrite the story of the city.

It's the task of the church to rewrite the story of the city. It's the task of the church to see beyond the problems in the city and see the promise over the city. Every city has promises. Every city is marked with a divine inscription. Our prophetic role involves more than condemning the darkness in our cities; we are to reveal the greatness obscured by the darkness. The church is called to make visible the beauty and glory of God already present in the city. We are called to drag divine promises to the surface.

God didn't call Jonah to take the city for Him. He called him to love the city with Him. "Should I not love that great city?"[3]

Scattered Servants Wash the Feet of the City

It's the privilege of the people of God to love their city back to life.

Parts of the church have confused bringing life to the city with taking our cities for God. In this worldview the city is an enemy, needing to be brought into subjection. We approach with a heart of militancy, not mercy. However, the posture of the church to the city is not as conqueror but as servant. The kingdom advances as we release compassion, not as we take dominion. We come not to take over our cities, but to lay our lives down.

God is more concerned with our posture toward our cities than our position in our cities. He is more concerned with our love for our cities than our leadership of our cities.[4] Our posture toward our cities is to be like Jesus. Just like Jesus, we show the fullness of our love for our cities by stooping low to wash the feet of the city. And just like Jesus approaching the city of Jerusalem, scattered servants show up in the city fully aware of their authority, yet clothed with humility and vulnerability. The goal is not to conquer the city but to create environments that love the city back to life.

Recall this description of Jesus as He entered the city of Jerusalem: "See, your king comes to you, gentle and riding on a donkey."[5] Scattered servants don't enter cities proclaiming victory; we come embracing vulnerability. We don't come in greatness; we come in weakness. As we humble our hearts, we don't make a big deal of what we are doing. We show up somewhere small and do something small, knowing we have nothing to prove and everything to give. We no longer try to be the biggest or best.

As Eric Swanson reminds us, it's only as we relinquish trying to be the best church *in* the city that we can reach toward the higher goal of becoming the best church *for* the city.[6] No longer scrambling for the "top of the mountain," we make ourselves of no reputation so we can wash the city's feet. We give ourselves to the lowest and the least.

Scattered servants don't take their cities for God. Scattered servants wash the feet of their cities with God.[7]

Scattered Servants Are Moved by the City

Scattered servants don't just move to the city as consumers. Scattered servants are moved by compassion for the city.

Many people move to the city to take from it rather than give to it. Careers are founded on such strategies and cities are broken by them. Moving to the city to access its resources and relationships may bring prosperity to us, but it never brings life to the city. It's not uncommon for twentysomethings to move to the city to fulfill their dreams without a thought of how their lives will add life to the city. The mind-set is one of extraction rather than servanthood. Take from the city what you can while you can.

It reminds me of the approach of the Prodigal Son. A young person living free from the constraints and control of home, he saw the city as a place where he could fulfill his destiny. The Prodigal Son used the city, but he never loved the city. It was a means to an end, a place with few boundaries, where self-expression and new experiences were the order of the day. In the eyes of the Prodigal, the city existed to feed his passions and his pleasures—to meet his needs. The city was a place where he could move from isolation to connection and then expansion. You can get everything and anything in the city. It's all available and accessible for consumption. So like everyone else, he consumed the opportunities presented by the city, took what he thought he needed to build his life, and missed the opportunity to lay down his life.

It's possible for churches to approach the city with the same mind-set. We gather people from the city but never really father the city. We use the city to build our churches but never really fall in love with the city.

But as Jesus approached Jerusalem and saw the city, He wept over it. He lamented the lack of peace in the city.

Scattered Servants Release Peace in the City

You can almost hear Jesus' heart breaking as He cries out, "If you, even you, had only known on this day what would bring you peace—but now it is hidden from your eyes."[8]

God is not at war with the city. He is for the city.

He desires that our cities be centers of peace. Therefore, in the Old Testament we are instructed to pray for the peace of our cities, to *request* peace for our cities. "Seek the peace of the city where I have caused you to be carried away captive, and pray to the LORD for it; for in its peace you will have peace."[9] However, in the New Testament we are not instructed to *request* peace for our cities; we are instructed to *release* peace on our cities. "Whatever city or town you enter … let your peace come upon it."[10] Our peace—the peace that rests upon and resides in a believer—has the capacity to reorder cities in accordance with the kingdom of God.

Usually we think of peace as tranquility, yet the biblical understanding of peace is transformative. The Hebrew word *shalom* implies expansive wholeness and goodness. It is a peace that propels us toward God's gloriously good future. It moves marriages, workplaces, and communities from deterioration to restoration, from decline into design.

This shalom/peace creates an environment where cities flourish. It reorders the environment to reflect the order of the kingdom. Therefore, the purpose of Christ's peace in our lives is not so we can live at ease but so we can bring release. When Jesus instructs us to allow our peace to rest upon (and thereby reorder) our cities, He invites us to bring transformation to areas of tension.

Parades are one of the areas of significant tension in Northern Ireland and in our community. Historically this single issue has torn at the heart of community in the city. Frequently they create division and escalate violence in the city. A stronger police presence often inflames the situation, and yet there must be presence to release order. This particular year, the police wanted to partner with voluntary agencies that might be able to help. So they invited our church to attend the parade. We inquired what they would like us to do. They responded, "When you show up, it changes the atmosphere." Imagine your city authorities saying that to your church.

Scattered servants do more than request peace for their cities. Scattered servants release peace on their cities.

The Prince of Peace lives in you. Therefore, you carry a peace that changes cities, reignites hope, and alters the trajectory of destinies.

As scattered servants we have the opportunity to *manifest* His peace so it is no longer hidden from the eyes of broken communities.

Scattered Servants Become Fathers to the City

The absence of peace in our cities is reflective of the absence of spiritual fathers. Where there are no "fathers," religion rules, shame rules, violence rules, addiction rules, dishonor rules. The city reels from a loss of identity, gives itself to trivialities, and misses its God-given destiny. Our cities struggle not because they lack guardians or governance, but because they lack fathers.[11]

As Paul said in 1 Corinthians 4:15, "Even if you had ten thousand guardians in Christ, you do not have many fathers." This statement, written centuries ago, could easily refer to our broken communities today.

Every city was founded by city fathers, and every city needs fathers to flourish. Individuals and cities mature into their destiny through fathers. These individuals affirm the good and the unique, breathe life and confidence into the city, draw out the hidden design, and release life into the community. Fathers are called to intentionally exercise their God-given influence to restore dignity, reveal design, release destiny in the city!

Agencies cannot replace fathers.

Governors cannot replace fathers.

Religion cannot replace fathers.

Policies cannot replace fathers.

Resources cannot replace fathers.

Churches cannot replace fathers.

So often, as communities of faith, we too have operated like the elder brother in our cities, comparing our lifestyle with the life of the city and entering into a posture of judgment. We have critiqued, complained, even condemned the city for its abuses, while we maintain a position of separatist obedience. Instead of understanding our role to supply the destiny of the city, we have maintained our distance from it.

Jesus appeared in the city to reveal the Father to the city.

It's time for the fathers to arise in the city.

Scattered Servants Partner with the City

Although scattered servants are sent as fathers, we don't come as know-it-alls but as give-it-alls. Our posture is not as experts but as explorers. We quickly discover our need of others. God's work in the city is always multiplied when the church is united. It's impossible to bring life to the community in isolation. We have to think holistically and partner intentionally. Not just partner *across* churches but partner *as* the church. As we have sought to lead the city into life at Causeway Coast Vineyard, we have found ourselves increasingly entering life-giving partnership not only with churches but with various charities and government agencies.

There are multiple agencies in the community—in business, education, health, government, media, and charity—that contribute significantly to the life of our city. We listen to them, learn from them, and lay down our lives with them. At times they lead us into the heart of the Father in ways we have never known or seen. Our shared commitment is to help make the community livable again, as all of us do whatever we can to supply the destiny of the community in creative and innovative ways. God has put enough in the city for the city. There is enough compassion, enough grace, enough resources, but no single church has it—not even a group of churches together has it. But together as a city we have enough for the city.

The Southampton Churches Network, led by my friend Billy Kennedy, is a wonderful example of how churches working together, partnering for the sake of the city, can rewrite the story. In recent years, this network has created public schools, advocated for adoption, alleviated areas of poverty, and worked with local politicians to bring life right where they are. These churches recognize that no single church has the solution for the city. No single church is given all of heaven's blueprint for the city. No single church has the relationships or resources to effect transformation in the city. It takes the whole church to change the city

A couple of years ago I attended Billy's thriving church. What caught my attention was the church's affection for the city and their decision to bless it. Hanging from the wall was the following sign:

> As we go out we are believing God for:
> Creative solutions to the city's challenges
> All areas of the city touched by God's presence
> A city of shelter for the refugee and stranger
> No violence or bloodshed
> The old and the young safe in the streets
> The lonely being placed in families
> A city of wisdom and sound mind

Faithful city, loving truth and justice
Known for peace and prosperity
Cities and nations coming here for God's blessing
Local and international businesses bringing in wealth
Young people arising and caring for nations
The city being glad as we are blessed by God.

Every Environment Alive in His Presence

We are beginning to witness this spirit in the arena of education. Initially, like most churches, our dream was to simply see kids encounter God. Not long after planting our church, we had the opportunity to conduct a mission in a school. We prepared for that time by praying and fasting throughout our small church. By the end of the week, twenty-eight kids had opened their lives to God. We considered it a remarkable and stunning week, and our pattern of interaction with schools continued in this vein. We would enter a school and help children encounter Christ. Others marveled at our effectiveness, yet inwardly we knew that nothing in the environment was changing. Lost souls were being found, but lost structures and systems remained unaffected and largely outside of our radar.

As I referenced in the last chapter, slowly the Father began to show us that it's more important to build a great city than to have a great church. We began to partner with other agencies in our city that were called to supply destiny too. We started to understand that schools and churches have the same goal when it comes to kids: namely unleashing them in their unique design and ultimate destiny. Suddenly we saw the school system as our partner in advancing the divine dream. Lost structures and systems were now firmly on our hearts because they were on His heart. We continued to operate multiple environments in schools, yet we changed our focus from running outreach programs for kids to serving and partnering with the school as a whole. How could we, as followers of Jesus, serve them as they served the city?

One school invited us to participate at their breakfast club, and several of our interns began showing up there each morning to serve the kids. They didn't talk about Jesus. They didn't have to. We didn't want them to—neither did the school. As trust developed, the school approached us requesting our assistance in mentoring some of the pupils during breaks. Essentially they were asking some of our team to spend time with the children. Again we agreed, thankful for the opportunity to serve while marveling at the grace of God that schools were actively seeking input from churches. Once more we didn't talk about Jesus; neither did we seek to promote the thirteen other environments we have for kids in church. We weren't using the school to build our church; we were using the church to build the school. Sure, inviting the kids would have boosted our attendance figures, but it wouldn't have changed the school. We were learning to be fathers in the city, supplying the destiny of key influencers in our city.

Recently the same school hosted their open evening for kids exploring secondary school options. They insisted that we be present because they wanted prospective pupils and their parents to know of our partnership in supplying pastoral care, in reducing bullying, in increasing the strength of the school academically. Since our partnership began, the school's rankings have changed for the better.

We can't really claim the credit. The truth is, it's a fabulous school changing young lives and instilling a hope and a future into the hearts of kids in our community. It's simply our privilege and honor to partner with them as they do it. Above that, we have the sense that who we are truly partnering with is the Father.

As we prayed about that partnership at our staff gathering recently, I almost heard the Father say, "Thank you. Thank you for loving the school and not just the schoolchildren. Thank you for caring about the structure and not only the souls. Thank you. My sons and daughters, as a result of their obedience to a dream I put in their heart, established many of the schools in your nation. They risked much and sacrificed greatly to see My dream come to pass. I care about what happens to the buildings, and I care about what happens to the system because I birthed the dream."

Their dream changed our city and now it's our turn to dream in ways that shape the city.

Chapter 14

DREAMS THAT SHAPE THE CITY

"You're crazy. This is *not* Hollywood."

It's a voice I have become accustomed to over the years. It's the voice that raises fears and silences dreams.

It came because over the last number of years we had prophesied and declared that our area would become a center for filmmaking. At the time it did seem ridiculous. We live in an obscure place about as far from Hollywood as possible. Nonetheless, we continued to stir up dreams in the hearts of people that God would ordain filmmakers here.

We had lots of reasons to doubt and few reasons to dream.

So we invited dreamers.

We confidently declared God was dreaming dreams over the whole of culture. The days were coming when we not only celebrated the dream of the young man on his way to Bible college, but we celebrated the dream of the young woman on her way to bring life to the fashion industry. The days were coming when pastors and filmmakers would be ordained together at the front of our churches. A shift was coming because dreamers were emerging.

Fast-forward six years, and increasingly films are being made in our area. These involve not only the amazing work of local writers and producers, but also internationally recognizable works such as *Game of Thrones* and the *Dracula* movie.

These are not the kinds of movies our folks will make. However, we know that those making the movies have to take a break sometime, and they have to eat somewhere. We also know that there are scattered servants all over our community and that nowhere is beyond reach of God's presence. Sooner or later, a film producer, or director, or actor is going to encounter life of another kind.

It's only a matter of time.

Our hope isn't merely changing the story of those involved in the industry. Our hope is that the story inscribed in our hearts would begin to be written everywhere on everything, in every corner of culture, and that new producers would emerge filled with the Spirit of God with access to the best ideas on the planet. They can lead the way in unleashing fresh creativity into decaying industries, cities, workplaces, and families.

Greg is a friend and one of those producers. He wrote this to me some time ago:

> Been to Causeway Coast Vineyard five times now
> over the last few months and am always so excited
> to come along. It's amazing to expect God to reveal
> Himself to us in the Holy Spirit—exciting and scary

and wonderful. I've been a Christian for most of my life, and this is a new experience for me. There's something I wanted to ask you about....

And so began a friendship and a journey together, believing it was possible to create something that could engage and change culture. Greg began to dream that people connected to the Creator could make the best TV programs. Later, Greg wrote:

Can't begin to describe this wonderful and beautiful creative journey. It is the best work I have ever created. I absolutely love this show. There's something special about this show. Many, many people have said that to me—they can see it. It's exactly like what you said to me the other day—that "thing" people recognise when we walk into a room. I know it's God's favor. I laid hands on the physical artwork and blessed it, asking the Father to do amazing things with it. He has been all over this, in every way and not least, the writing. It's those stories of hope. They carry the values, the heart of the Father.

Against all odds and with no experience of doing so, I've sold it to the US, UK, Australia, all of Scandinavia, Israel, and we've news that most of the rest of the world will take it—from Japan to Iceland. I asked God to open broadcasters in every country in the world so that every child with a television would be able to see these stories.

And to think he almost became a youth pastor. There is nothing wrong with being a pastor ... except when you are called to be a filmmaker.

Kingdom Culture Is Full of Dreamers

It's more important to empower people to bring life to culture than to enlist people who support church structures. It's more important to call out the dreamer-over-the-city than recruit people to serve our ministry. When our dreams center upon the church, we confine the dreamers in the church. Instead of catalyzing kingdom dreamers, we neutralize them. Our problem isn't that people are falling asleep *at* church, but that people have fallen asleep *as* church. And who can blame them? We are mind-numbingly bored of religious services that have little impact on cities.[1] We were made to be dreamers and visionaries.

Kingdom culture is full of dreamers. It's the overspill of the Spirit of God in our lives. The Spirit of wisdom and revelation releases dreams all over the city.[2] So whenever God wants to change a city, He summons dreamers. He declares in essence, "Let there be artists, and let them create stunning works of beauty that evoke wonder. Let there be businessmen, and let them see the people beyond the profit, and introduce ideas that steward life. Let there be families, and let glory reside in them and among them. Let them be marked by honor. Let there be medics, and let them pioneer breakthroughs and advances that trample on the head of disease."

This dreaming-over-the-city is what believers are supposed to do. More than that, it's in our spiritual DNA. God promised His community would be dreamers and visionaries.

In the last days, God says,
 I will pour out my Spirit on all people.
Your sons and daughters will prophesy,
 your young men will see visions,
 your old men will dream dreams.
Even on my servants, both men and women,
 I will pour out my Spirit in those days,
 and they will prophesy.[3]

In the last days God is raising up believers who move beyond the needs of the church and begin to dream over their cities—dreams that shape the city. He promises: "I will pour out My Spirit on all flesh and dreamers will arise. You'll no longer be limited to what you could do in your own power. A dream will ignite within you. Young men will dream dreams. Old men will have visions." Young men dream beyond their generation and old men live for more than they have seen. The hallmark of the Spirit resting on us is dreams that are bigger than us.

Dave and Emily moved from Dublin to our town several years ago. They were gifted, brilliant young adults who dreamed of making a difference with their lives. So they joined our staff team. It wasn't long before ministries around them flourished. Yet within them burned another dream—the creation of a space in our community where lost and found could gather. It would also be a space where their passion for coffee and good food would flourish. So without business experience, they listened to their desires, transitioned from our staff, and pursued the dream.

As a church we sent them out to plant their business, and the café Lost & Found was born. Dave and Emily intentionally situated their café in one of the more dilapidated areas of our community, but it wasn't long before the quality of their business attracted other business. Estate agents talked about the atmosphere of the area being altered and the desirability of hosting offices on businesses on that street now that Lost & Found was present.

At the Irish Restaurant Awards Ceremony in 2017, Lost & Found was declared to be the best café in the whole of Ireland. It may sound like a dream come true, but Dave and Emily are dreaming a bigger dream, beyond what they have seen God do so far. As they say on their website, "Lost & Found is a community and family of people who carry a different narrative from the culture around them. Our aim is to fuel the dreams of those around us, to encourage and empower people to live a better story. At the core of Lost & Found is the belief that we all need places of community, and today more than ever. We want L&F to be a creative space for our community to eat, drink, talk and dream."

Unoriginal Sin and Original Design

We never used to dream God-sized dreams for our city. We used to distrust our dreams.

We were more aware of the doctrine of original sin than the discovery of original design. Therefore, we assumed if a desire originated in our hearts, it probably wasn't good enough to be in God's heart. So we focused on denying our desires, downplaying and downsizing our dreams. It seemed like the faithful thing to do. But it was frustrating. It always is when we try to live a New Testament lifestyle with an Old Testament mind-set. It only ever produces passivity and futility.

The apostle Paul addresses this dilemma when he says:

> As for you, you were dead in your transgressions and sins, in which you used to live when you followed the ways of this world and of the ruler of the kingdom of the air, the spirit who is now at work in those who are disobedient. All of us also lived among them at one time, gratifying the cravings of our flesh and following its desires and thoughts. Like the rest, we were by nature deserving of wrath. But because of his great love for us, God, who is rich in mercy, made us alive with Christ even when we were dead in transgressions—it is by grace you have been saved. And God raised us up with Christ and seated us with him in the heavenly realms in Christ Jesus, in order that in the coming ages he might show the incomparable riches of his grace, expressed in his kindness to us in Christ Jesus.[4]

The Living Bible translation phrases it this way: "You went along with the crowd and you were just like all the others." You were just like everyone else. You didn't understand your uniqueness. You lived according to the pattern of this world without any revelation that God had put a unique desire and a unique dream within you. Instead of forming dreams that transformed the city, you followed dreams that were in the world. Whatever you saw other people desire, you gave yourself to that desire. Your dreams were rooted in comparison rather than compassion.

Once you went along with the crowd and were just like all the others. It was impossible for you to live expansively and creatively. You were locked into the opinions and the outcomes of others, just expressing the evil within, incapable of releasing irreversible good. Unoriginal sin: simply following the trend instead of setting the standard. Your dreams were rooted in tradition, not revelation.

But God, who is rich in mercy, gave us back our lives again.[5] God made us alive in Christ.

Now in Christ, we have been drafted into a greater dream that leads us beyond ourselves into God's pattern and plan for bringing all things under heaven and earth under one head—even Christ. We have been drawn into a dream that is creative, redemptive, expansive, and generous. We are released *from* the pattern of this world to create a pattern *for* this world.

Cultivate Courageous Dreams and Courageous Dreamers

In Christ, the dream that has been there all along, even though it may have been buried under disappointment and difficulty, suddenly comes alive. Alive with His life. His design fills our spiritual DNA.

Yet without awareness of the dreams God has wired into our spiritual DNA, we tend to reach for what has been instead of what could be. We settle for repeating history instead of rewriting history. Many settle for *covetous* dreams rather than *courageous* dreams. Covetous dreams have zero potential to awaken cities as they reduce our capacity to the scale of what already exists. Courageous dreamers refuse to settle for a little more of what everyone else has; they press on to introduce those things that have never been seen.

Courageous dreams emerge through immersion in the presence. Yet they can't stay there. They must engage.

I love the story of C. S. Lewis sitting in an Oxford chapel, soaking in the presence, expressing his desires before God. As Lewis exits the church, there's a door directly across from the church with a lion's face etched into it. And beside it were little sculptures of Mr. Tumnus. As C. S. Lewis walks out of church to begin his ordinary everyday life, having connected and celebrated with God, he looks at a door, and a whole new world is born. Suddenly, he is writing book after book that will change children's lives for generations to come. His contemplation in the sanctuary led to imagination for society.

It happened as he came out of church.

The dreams of God lie just beyond the doors of our churches, but we never see them emerge unless we immerse our desires in His presence.

The Desire of Our Hearts

God didn't just write His laws into our hearts through the New Covenant; He put His life in us. Therefore, our desires change to reflect the nature of God; our dreams change to carry the purposes of God. Ezekiel prophesied this reality:

> I will give you a new heart and put a new spirit in
> you. Your new heart comes from my heart. I will
> rewire you with my desires and dreams. Your new

heart is not like your old heart. Your old heart was
rebellious but your new heart will be responsive
because I will remove from you your heart of stone
and give you a heart of flesh. And I will put my
Spirit in you and move you to follow my decrees
and be careful to keep my laws. I will put a new
direction in your life and a new permission.[6]

"The entire focus of our faith has been the elimination of
wrong desires. That is important, but there is a greater reality—the
unleashing of heavenly desire in the nations."[7] Jesus dwells in our
hearts and He has written His desires there. When we cut off the
inflow of God's creativity in our lives in the name of humility, we
live lives of frustration, futility, and passivity. Not every desire is part
of God's design. But when we dream according to God's design, we
infect our communities with lasting hope.

This is one reason Paul prays that God would fulfill our good
desires and bring them to fruition.

[I pray] that by his power he may bring to fruition
your every desire for goodness and your every deed
prompted by faith. We pray this so that the name
of our Lord Jesus may be glorified in you, and you
in him, according to the grace of our God and the
Lord Jesus Christ.[8]

Isn't that a subversive prayer? It uproots our religious mind-set. It
should read "by His power God would fulfill every good purpose of

HIS."[9] But Paul prays that God would fill and fulfill every good desire of the believers. God is so generous that He pours His power on *our* good desires. He invites us to share our dreams and desires with Him, and then in His power He comes upon us to implement them.

We find an example of this in Luke's gospel. "Therefore, since I myself have carefully investigated everything from the beginning ... it seemed good also to me, to write an orderly account."[10] Luke woke up one day and had the idea to write a book. It just seemed good to him. It was his desire. His initiative. Luke didn't know he was writing a gospel. He was writing out of the overflow of his interests. And so it was that a doctor with a passion for history became an author.

Nowhere does it say God instructed him to write the book. Yet it later became clear that God inspired the book. Luke loved to write, and as he did what he loved, God breathed on it. When God by His power brought to fruition Luke's good desire, it changed nations for generations. Still today lives are changed as they encounter the words written by Luke.

You have permission to create out of your God-given passion. When you do what you love, you come alive. And when you come alive, you begin to fulfill the very purpose that God has for you. While God can and does download desires and dreams from heaven, His greatest pleasure is fulfilling the desire of our hearts. This partnership is glorious to Him.[11]

Permission to Dream

Although kingdom ideas can be downloaded, they are often discovered. When God begins to bring greater life to the city, He looks at what we have in our hearts, not what we have in our hands. He partners with us to bring life to the city.

One night, King Solomon went to sleep, and as he slept, God visited him in a dream. "At Gibeon the LORD appeared to Solomon during the night in a dream, and God said, 'Ask for whatever you want me to give you.'"[12] There was no restriction on what Solomon could ask. There was no instruction for what Solomon should ask. There *was* invitation for Solomon to discover the desire in his heart and speak it out. "Ask for whatever you want." Whatever is written in your heart today will be written in your nation tomorrow.

Although he was asleep, Solomon was awake to what God had already written into his heart for the sake of the city and for the sake of God's glory. Solomon knew his one great desire: wisdom. Wisdom to draw out the dreams of others. Wisdom to govern the people whom God had destined for greatness. While most people dream of having more, Solomon dreamed of giving more.

> Solomon answered, "You have shown great kindness to your servant, my father David, because he was faithful to you and righteous and upright in heart. You have continued this great kindness to him and have given him a son to sit on his throne this very day. "Now, LORD my God, you have made your servant king in place of my father David. But I am only a little child and do not know how to carry out my duties. Your servant is here among the people you have chosen, a great people, too numerous to count or number. So give your servant a [wise

and] discerning heart to govern your people and to distinguish between right and wrong. For who is able to govern this great people of yours?"[13]

While God could have told Solomon what he needed, He wanted to see what Solomon desired. Solomon's dream and desire of bringing life to others captivated the heart of God. "The LORD was pleased that Solomon had asked for this."[14] That is code for: Solomon's desire was filled with God's delight. It ravished His heart. So God determined to bring to fruition Solomon's every desire for goodness.

God said to him, "Since you have asked for this and not for long life or wealth for yourself, nor have asked for the death of your enemies but for discernment in administering justice, I will do what you have asked. I will give you a wise and discerning heart."[15]

In effect, God says that since your desire was for the sake of the city, since your dream was to serve the destiny of the nation and not for self-preservation or promotion, "I will give you a wise and discerning heart."[16] God exposed the desire of Solomon's heart so that He could empower the desire of Solomon's heart. So that Solomon could do the good works God prepared in advance for him to do.

Good Works Prepared in Advance for Us

The Bible calls it the good works God prepared in advance for us to do. The works God wrote into our heart long ago. "For we are God's handiwork, created in Christ Jesus to do good works, which God prepared in advance for us to do."[17]

You are engraved by the very hand of God. God's hand reached into your life and inscribed something unique on your soul the moment you were conceived. He wrote His dreams into your core. He inscribed something unique in you that the world has never seen before. And if you knew what He had for your life, you would never be jealous of anyone else. God in heaven has entered your life to make a difference beyond your life, and that difference is meant to spill out everywhere on everything. We are His workmanship, created in Christ Jesus to do good works. You are uniquely wired by God to dream according to His design and unleash His creativity in our communities.

But God will not do them without us. They are good works for *us* to do. God has deliberately limited Himself, restrained Himself, so that we can experience the joy of dreaming and doing together with Him. "God works together with those who love him to release what is good."[18] We know that in *everything* God works together with those who love Him to release what is good. Now, to make this idea more specific, try saying it this way:

We know that in politics, God works together with those who love Him to release what is good.

We know that in medicine, God works together with those who love Him to release what is good.

We know that in finding a cure for cancer, God works together with those who love Him to release what is good.

We know that in wealth creation, God works together with those who love Him to release what is good.

We know that in entrepreneurial thinking, God works together with those who love Him to release what is good.

We know that in developing technologies that reduce poverty, God works together with those who love Him to release what is good.

With this in mind, we enter our cities praying, "Father, help us to work with You to release what is good for the city. Give us wisdom and revelation into who You are and what You have given us so that it utterly changes who we are and what we are for. Grant us insight into Your purpose and help us take initiative in bringing it to pass. We give ourselves to that wholeheartedly. Give us the audacity to believe that there are greater things still to come, greater things still to be done in the city."[19]

God has *prepared* good works in advance for us to do.

These good works are not somewhere in heaven waiting to be prayed down. They are hidden in our hearts waiting to spring up. There are also things He has hidden in the heart of your community that will only be released when you come along and align yourself with them. There are families without purpose, marriages without passion, businesses without direction, communities without hope needing to be reminded of their design. They are waiting for someone to remind them that this is not all they were made for, that God in heaven has drafted them into the divine dream that awakens them to their eternal purpose.

God has prepared good works in advance for us to *do*.

We have the assignment to invade the realms of society in a way that brings the kingdom. When this text gets hold of us and we get hold of it, we begin seeking to see the wisdom of God so infiltrate our lives that it makes an impact on our cities. We begin to wonder what it would look like if the wisdom of God were turned loose. The divine dream begins spilling out. We understand that the call to go after the lost includes the redemptive dream not only for souls but also for cities. God has prepared good works for us to do in our cities as well as our churches. He has divine desires and dreams that every environment in our city would come alive to His presence.

You Are the Light of the World

I stood before our congregation as I had done many years before when declaring we would see one hundred people come to faith. This time the declaration wasn't about people coming to faith or church. This time there was no declaration, only a question: What do you think God dreams of over this city?

The greatest advancements in medicine are yet to happen.

The best politicians are yet to emerge.

The best economies and economic models are yet to be built.

The best artists who will paint and sculpt some of the best artistic designs are yet to come.

It's time to dream dreams that shape the city.

The dream of God over your life is not that you become a believer and help out the local church. The dream of God over your life is that you come alive in His presence and bring life to every environment, spilling contagious hope into hurting humanity. God has entrusted believers with an assignment to lead the earth into life. We must pursue that which God has given us for the transformation of the nations. We must unleash the unique blueprint of God for our lives and our community in a creative, expansive, and imaginative way. And we must not call arrogance what God has called obedience, even if everyone else labels it arrogance. It's not arrogance to take our place in the city—it's obedience in what we are supposed to do.

Jesus didn't enter your life so that you could attend a church and contribute to a ministry. Jesus entered your story so that together with Him you could go rewrite the story of everything, everywhere. That is your calling; that is your task; that is your assignment.

You are the light of the world.

It is time to let our light shine, to demonstrate original design. It is time to show that God isn't just good at religion or spiritual things. Our God is good at everything. He's good at medicine and innovation. He's good at filmmaking and a master of art. He's a bestselling author and an amazing sculptor. He has all these ways to bring hope to town, and He is summoning His dreamers now. And they're dreaming wild dreams … over all of creation, every area of culture!

Chapter 15

CULTURE CARRIERS

I had been wrestling with the text for months. I still didn't believe it.

I assented to it intellectually. But I didn't believe it. It was in the Scripture. It just wasn't in culture.

So I read it again.

> Thanks be to God, who in Christ always leads us in triumphal procession, and through us spreads the fragrance of the knowledge of him everywhere.[1]

Everywhere? Through us?

I still couldn't take it in. So I did what I do when a text disrupts my world. I poured out my prayer. "Father, I believe that Christ is exalted over all things. He has triumphed over the powers of darkness. I believe that He leads us into everything You have for us. And I believe that You have empowered the church. But I don't yet believe that through us You spread *everywhere* the knowledge of the fragrance of Christ. Because if that were true, then where are the Christian politicians setting the agenda in our culture and our community? Where are the nurses and the doctors who are Christians who are pioneering exceptional breakthroughs in the areas of medicine?"

Still the word haunted me. *Everywhere.*

If God's desire is to spread *everywhere* the fragrance of the knowledge of Christ, then it's clear He wants to do a whole lot more with His church than we've ever given Him credit for. It's clear He wants to send His church into places that we've never, ever dreamed possible—and places we've deliberately avoided.

No Longer Intimidated by Culture

It's impossible to receive our inheritance in culture when we practice avoidance of culture. Our cultural avoidance is rooted in a letter written to the cultural epicenter of an empire. What happened in Rome was exported everywhere.

> Therefore, I urge you, brothers and sisters, in view of God's mercy, to offer your bodies as a living sacrifice, holy and pleasing to God—this is your true and proper worship. Do not conform to the pattern of this world, but be transformed by the renewing of your mind. Then you will be able to test and approve what God's will is—his good, pleasing and perfect will.[2]

Do not conform to the pattern of this world.

Sadly, we made the text about *avoiding* the world when it's really about *altering* the world. Historically, we thought the way to stay out of conformity was to stay out of community—to avoid culture entirely. We created rules and rhythms for our lives that involved disengagement from culture. We wrongly assumed the prevailing culture was more contagious than the average believer. So we stayed clear. We practiced cultural avoidance in the hope it would result in sin avoidance.

But the text is about so much more than sin avoidance; it is about releasing kingdom abundance.

Paul wrote to believers in the cultural epicenter of his day and invited them to be immersed in the divine presence in a way that made a difference to the superpower of their day. Paul believed that societal shifts were possible—that it was possible for cities, even nations, to come under the influence of the kingdom.

Paul's argument is that our regeneration becomes *the* sign of re-creation of everything. The divine mercy that transformed us forbids us then to conform to any other story. Mercy has brought us into the life-giving story, the living story. Therefore, since mercy has rewritten our story, we have a different mentality, and a greater capacity to rewrite the story of our cities and communities. God is bringing everything under one head. Sooner or later, the whole of history and all of humanity end up at the feet of Jesus.

Do not conform to the pattern of this world ... introduce another world. Introduce the solutions of the future.

Conformity is a sin for believers because our mandate is to transform culture. You are called to steward kingdom solutions, to live an uncommon life, to recognize that there is something resting on you that resets the world around you. It has the capacity to change everything, the capacity to change everywhere, the capacity to change everyday. You were put on earth to establish some things and to abolish some things. You are alive today not to conform but to bring reformation to something. You are alive today to rewrite the story of some town, of some region, of some nation, somewhere. Of everything, everywhere.

The church is not intimidated by culture. We are inscribing resurrection life into culture.

Everything, Everywhere

This has been the divine dream all along. Believers of all nations and generations have always known it to be so. We have this God-honoring, life-stretching desire to see every area of our cities and our cultures infected with His goodness and glory. We have the insatiable, even inescapable, desire to see our families and our communities experience the influence of generous hope. It may seem crazy, but changing the world is our family business.

> All this energy issues from Christ: God raised him
> from death and set him on a throne in deep heaven,
> in charge of running the universe, everything from
> galaxies to governments, no name and no power
> exempt from his rule. And not just for the time
> being, but *forever*. He is in charge of it all, has the

final word on everything. At the center of all this, Christ rules the church. The church, you see, is not peripheral to the world; the world is peripheral to the church. The church is Christ's body, in which he speaks and acts, by which he fills everything with his presence.[3]

He fills everything in every way through His church.

Substitute the word *everything* with the word *culture*. Through His church, He fills culture with His presence. The church fulfills its mandate when it fills society, not when it fills the sanctuary. The Scriptures teach us that it's through the body of Jesus—scattered throughout society—that God fills "everything, everywhere" with His presence. This "everything, everywhere" includes our homes, offices, schools, restaurants, and streets. God's heart is that our society—not just our services—would be full of His life. God's desire is to draw the entire city—every heart and every home—into His hope, His inheritance, and His power.

Substitute the word *everything* there with the word *city*. Through His church, He fills the city in every way for His glory. God's glory filling the city—your city. His glory fills the city as we live out our story in the city. Although it's possible for God to gloriously invade a city, He has chosen to infiltrate the city through ordinary believers who live in His presence and live out their influence. It *is* through *us* that He spreads the fragrance of the knowledge of Him everywhere. The divine dream of everything, everywhere filled with His presence is released as we unleash everyone, everywhere, everyday.

Scattered Servants Are Culture Carriers

The Spirit rests on you to release the city. You are the culture carrier; you are the contaminator; you are the one called by God to bring life. Therefore, you have the holy, honorable task of reversing decline and releasing design again into your streets, schools, businesses, families, colleges, and communities. Avoiding culture is simply not an option for kingdom carriers. There is a world out there longing for the kingdom that is alive in us.[4]

Like many parts of Scandinavia, Sweden is primarily a secular culture. Sadly, the church there has been in decline for many years. As a result, many local churches are imprisoned in a survivor mind-set. Insecurity rather than authority marks their engagement with their community and there is little expectation of kingdom outpouring. So the idea that people who were far from God would take a seat in public to receive prayer seems inconceivable.

Against this backdrop, our church hosted a conference involving various leaders from Denmark, Finland, Norway, and Sweden. For many, it was their first encounter with our Healing on the Streets model. Understandably, they came with the usual insecurities, but as the weekend progressed, they began to gain fresh insight into their authority and recover their voice. One afternoon, seven teams traveled to different areas of the city of Uppsala. My team was assigned to an area known as the ghetto. This caused great excitement in our hearts because we know that God always pours out His favor on the marginalized.

We arrived wondering what to expect. We didn't have to wait long to find out. The first person to take a seat was a Muslim gentleman who had fought in Iraq and sustained an injury where shrapnel had lodged in his spine. As a result, he was in considerable discomfort and searching for relief. In the middle of the ghetto, the church stepped out of its cultural ghetto and began demonstrating the kingdom with hospitality and generosity.

Unsurprisingly, a few moments later the man signaled to his friend that he had been healed, and then his friend took a seat and poured out his complaint. We spent around ninety minutes praying for people (mostly Muslims), during which time we witnessed several people receive healing. One man shook violently in his chair as the Spirit of God fell upon him and healed his disease. When we returned to report this to the rest of the conference, we were delighted (and not at all surprised) to hear that every other team had similar stories of kingdom compassion.

As one homeless man was being prayed for in a local park, a lady on the team had a distinct picture of his foot standing on a broken bottle. She inquired whether he had sustained such an injury. At this point he promptly removed his socks and shoes to reveal the scar where the bottle had pierced his foot. He was so profoundly touched that God knew his condition that he opened his life to Christ in that moment. In the evening he came to the leaders conference, thrilled as others shared the story of his journey.

His, of course, was not the only story. One after another, people rose to share their experiences of what happened on the streets. Each team had encountered the kingdom and spoke about the joy that had come to the city that day. In total, fifty-six people had instantly been healed. It was a beautiful moment depicting what God does when the church rediscovers its voice, no longer intimidated by the prevailing culture, and daring to enter the community.

Scattered servants are culture carriers. When culture carriers enter the prevailing culture, everything shifts. The Spirit rests on us to release the city.

Renew the Culture by Releasing the Kingdom

Our assignment to change the world around us can't happen through abandonment of culture. It happens through engagement with culture. However, engaging is different from imitating. Imitation of culture leads to imprisonment in culture.

Remember Paul's words: "Do not conform any longer to the pattern of this world." Today he might write, "Don't allow your values for excellence to move too far into desperate attempts for cultural relevance. Don't you realize that relevance to a decaying culture is a vote for death?" Kingdom culture is released through kingdom resonance, not cultural relevance.

Yet large parts of the church today have sacrificed the release of kingdom culture on the altar of cultural relevance. Not so the church of the future. The church of the future will neither practice cultural avoidance nor hunger for cultural relevance. It will no longer be intimidated or impressed by culture. Churches in the future will know that we can't bring life to the city by avoiding the city or by becoming the city. The church of the future will move beyond seeking cultural relevance toward releasing culture.

Cultural relevance is too low a goal. Cultural renewal is our family business.

The Spirit rests on us to transform the city, not perform for the city. God has not called us to cultural relevance, but to cultural renaissance. He has called us to create culture and shape culture that will lead society into a new story, into full humanity, into the glory He ordained from the beginning. We don't do that by becoming like the culture; we do that by carrying the culture of the kingdom and helping the culture step into a new identity. We renew the culture through releasing the kingdom.

Our Mandate Is Cultural Renewal

It's impossible to bring life to culture by becoming like the culture. Our calling is not to sit at the feet of culture and learn, but to lift up our voices within culture and lead. What the Spirit forms in the church resonates with the culture. Just like the day the church was formed.

Suddenly a sound came from heaven and reverberated in the surrounding community.[5] The church was propelled beyond the building as it recognized and responded to the sound from heaven.[6] It wasn't trying to connect with culture or relate to culture. It was moving with a move of God, and as a result, people gathered from everywhere because they had never heard or seen such a thing.

The early church didn't import existing culture into the church; they exported kingdom culture to the world.

It's what culture carriers do.

We no longer confine our creative expression to singing in our services, skillful dramas, brilliant videos, painting prophetically, or dancing at the front of church. Rather, we understand our role in releasing writers, sculptors, poets, and filmmakers into creative engagement that piques curiosity within the wider culture.

If God has called you to be an artist, for God's sake, be an artist. But don't hide it in church. Take it to the city, do an art exhibition in your city, release it in your city. If God has empowered you to express His life through art, then become portable with your art. Take your art out of the building. Take it into the culture and let people see it. Let broken humanity wonder with curiosity at the divine beauty, the divine story that is revealed and released through your art.

One day a young woman in our church approached me. She felt that her primary expression of worship happened through dance and wanted to serve our church by occasionally dancing onstage as part of our services. She could tell by my face that I wasn't enthusiastic about the idea. Yet my reply still shocked her. I said, "We don't do that here." She said, "You don't? Then what do I do? I think God has called me to dance." The look on her face conveyed her thoughts: *Are you really going to squash what God's calling on my life? Are you going to be another controlling leader?* I continued, "Are you sure God has called you to dance?" She said, "God's called me to dance!" I said, "Well, if God really has called you to dance, why would you settle for a nine-foot stage on a Sunday? If the living God has called you to dance, why don't you go into the community and set up dance schools for kids?" She was frustrated and slightly mad at me. But today she owns a thriving dance school in our community with a significant waiting list. It's not surprising. God has called her to dance!

If God has called you to dance, then for God's sake, dance. But don't only perform your dance routines in church; transform the dreams of young dancers in the city. Scattered servants do not *conform* to the pattern of the culture, and they do not *perform* according to the pattern of the culture.

Living in His Presence, Living Out Our Brilliance

I love how Bill Johnson paraphrases the Romans 12 passage, "Be transformed by the renewing of your mind, so that you can communicate and demonstrate the solutions from another world."[7] A renewed mind doesn't only give us a renewed worldview; it overflows into a renewed world. It enables us to demonstrate heaven's solutions and kingdom inventions in media, arts, education, finance, government, sport, film, relationships … in every area of culture. Transformed minds discern and demonstrate original design in culture. As our minds are transformed, we have a capacity to think differently. Since we are no longer enslaved by our old ways of thinking, we can bring an alternative story, an innovative story—a story immersed in heaven's reality, covered in mercy, and setting captives free.

Renewed minds renew culture.

Believers with a renewed mind move from trying to be trendy to being authentically innovative. They live in resonance with the culture of heaven. Our transformed mind leads to tomorrow's world. Therefore, we no longer look at the music charts as the source of our inspiration. Instead, we practice bold creativity because we are unleashing something into the earth that has never existed before. We live in creative resonance, doing what our Father is doing, releasing what He is releasing. We demonstrate and communicate solutions from another world.

It's time to demonstrate divine design. It's time to live in His presence and live out our brilliance. It's time to bring out the God colors in culture. It's time to stop sitting at the feet of culture and begin shaping culture. And it's time to do it beyond the building, rewriting the story of our city in a thousand innovative, imaginative ways.

And then watch: what God incubates in the hearts of trusted rulers will resonate with the dreams and needs of the city.

Exposing the Brilliance of God to Surrounding Culture

God gave Solomon wisdom, and Solomon released original design using the wisdom God gave. Solomon created a culture where the solutions of God were seen, welcomed, and embraced. The wisdom became inherent in the culture to such an extent that the surrounding cultures began to gather. The queen of Sheba, a powerful ruler of an empire, traveled great distances to see the brilliance of God exhibited in Solomon's world.[8] When we bring to our city the insight, innovations, and improvements God has in mind, our cities begin to respond positively and invite our influence.

King Solomon didn't avoid culture, he shaped culture. He did so through the dreams and desires God had placed in his heart. He wasn't impressed by culture or intimidated by culture; he was influencing culture and inviting it into life. And he did it everyday. Everyday Solomon unleashed the arts: poetry, paintings, songs. He increased knowledge: science, industry, and botany. He invented, engineered, innovated, and improved all aspects of culture. He set the standard for excellence through kingdom influence. Solomon did more than imitate the dreams of those before him or those around him. He went beyond them.

In the future, the church will be at the heart of creativity in the city, bringing creative solutions to perennial problems. It will pulsate with innovative and generative ideas, bringing fresh life to the city as it resounds with wisdom.

Insights. Ingenuity. Inventions. Innovations. Exposing the brilliance of God to surrounding culture will change the world.

Introducing and Innovating the Future

It's happened before.

The Renaissance was a period when the posture of exploration and discovery marked our engagement with culture. The church excelled in thinking with God and imagining with Him. Sadly we gradually traded discovery for doctrine, innovation for imposition. Now we have largely neglected, even forsaken, the work of kingdom imagination. Yet God created us with imagination, and He longs to bring us to His imagineering room. "Now to him who is able to do immeasurably more than all we ask or imagine, according to his power that is at work within us."[9]

This text is not saying don't even bother trying to imagine; it's actually an encouragement into a sanctified imagination, an imagination under the influence of the Spirit of God. We have trusted the ability of the enemy to corrupt our imagination and dishonored the desire of our Father to fill up our imagination.

While many churches find themselves somewhere on the spectrum between "intimidation by" and "imitation of" the culture around them, effective churches are those who imagine with God and "innovate within" their culture. They are the church inspiring the city, breathing life into every area of decay by breathing out the God-filled life within them. Inspiring churches are more than models for other churches; they are movements of hope in the midst of brokenness.

Innovative churches don't simply restructure services; they restore cities. These churches influence the city through the sacrificial involvement of scattered servants—everyday, everywhere. Instead of retreating, they permeate every corner of the city, every area of culture, discovering the imaginative God already at work, and partnering with Him there. Innovative churches introduce the future more than the city could ever imagine on its own. Innovative churches are inventive, creative, and expansive pictures of the future. Their presence is to reveal and reflect God's abundance for that city.

Imagine what would happen if the local church took its creative abilities—music, storytelling, songwriting, art, filmmaking—out of the realm of private thoughts or corporate gatherings, and released them into the arena of public hope. What might happen as the church recovered its voice and its confidence?

Imagine the church in your city commissioning filmmakers, business leaders, artists, and educators, joined together to shape the city through prophetic imagination. Imagine the local church becoming the creative center and innovative capital of your city. Imagine if—through the integrity, involvement, and inventions of the local church—the glory of God was revealed to and released for your city.

Imagine a new renaissance!

All Things New

"And I heard a loud voice from the throne saying, 'Look! God's dwelling place is now among the people, and he will dwell with them. They will be his people, and God himself will be with them and be their God. "He will wipe every tear from their eyes. There will be no more death" or mourning or crying or pain, for the old order of things has passed away.' He who was seated on the throne said, 'I am making everything new!'"[10]

God is making all things new *right now*, not at some distant point in the future. This is the central message of the Revelation. It's the idea that God in the middle of chaos is already breaking through—already transforming communities and cities. It's a large vision and a huge mystery. Most of all, it is comprehensive mercy. God isn't just making everyone nice; He is making everything new.

Jesus speaks and says, "I am making all things new." It's one thing to have a vision for your city; it's another thing when God's voice breaks in upon your city and begins declaring, "I am making all things new."

This making-all-things-new has always been our story. You could be forgiven for thinking that the goal of our faith is moral improvement, cleaning up character, but it's so much deeper, so much wider, so much greater. He is making everything new. Not just religious things but everything.

He is making engineering new.

He is making architecture new.

He is making new sounds and colors.

He is making economies new and industries new.

He is doing it in churches, and He is doing it in the city.

The church you see is not peripheral to the culture; it's essential for the culture. You are a city on a hill. You are the light of the world. Raised up in the city; raised up for the city. The city doesn't make sense without the church, and the church doesn't make sense without the city. We are made visible to show forth a model of cultural renewal.

The very existence of the church is the evidence that the kingdom is come near and all things are being made new. You have been fighting for your corner in culture, but divine glory will cover culture. God is telling us, "I am making all things new. It's what I have always done. I spoke the word that gave birth to the world. I sent My Son to bring life to the world. I set My Spirit in My church to share everything Christ has made available. And this Holy Spirit will teach you all things … because He is brilliant at everything."

For years we have kept Him in our buildings and we have used Him in our services, but we have forgotten Him in our industries and our universities. Nevertheless, He is making all things new and He is moving once again. And the next great move of God is not going to be a movement *in* the church. It's going to be a movement *of* the church *into* society, rewriting the story of every aspect of our cities—everyone, everywhere, everyday—communicating, demonstrating, and celebrating the supremacy of Christ in every corner of culture.

Because He is making all things new.

ACKNOWLEDGMENTS

My humble gratitude goes out to …

John Scott, Mark Marx: "In those days mighty warriors roamed the earth." Your example, encouragement, and resilient faith have indelibly marked my life. Thank you for reaching for the impossible and refusing to settle for anything else.

Staff of Causeway Coast Vineyard: Your willingness to journey into unchartered territory and ability to lead generously shaped much of my journey. Thanks for doing whatever it takes to bring life to the city. It is an honor to know you and to have served with you.

David C Cook publishers: Thanks for providing the push needed to make sure this book saw the light of day. I am grateful for your partnership and editorial skills.

Sophie and Emily: Heart of my own heart whatever befall. You are the joy and delight of my life. Thanks for the sacrifices you made to give me space to write. And for your willingness to take the next step into the story of God.

To my wife, Kathryn: You are God's greatest gift in my life, anchoring my heart in hope and teaching me how to love. Your delight in sacrificing your dreams to release life in others taught us what it means to wash the feet of the city. Thank you.

NOTES

Chapter 1

1. Paraphrased from the book *Power through Prayer* by E. M. Bounds. The full quote reads, "We are constantly on a stretch, if not on a strain, to devise new methods, new plans, new organizations to advance the Church and secure enlargement and efficiency for the gospel. This trend of the day has a tendency to lose sight of the man or sink the man in the plan or organization. God's plan is to make much of the man, far more of him than of anything else. Men are God's method. The Church is looking for better methods; God is looking for better men."

2. Acts 8:8 tells us that when scattered servants showed up in Samaria, there was great joy in the city.

Chapter 2

1. 2 Samuel 12:8b.
2. Matthew 4:23.
3. Matthew 15:30–31 THE MESSAGE.
4. Acts 5:12–16.
5. Acts 5:19–20.
6. Matthew 9:35–38.
7. Acts 6:8.
8. Psalm 77:14.

9. Psalm 96:3.

10. In a humorous note to his brother Charles, John Wesley chided and reminded him not to permit the vast crowds of people to climb the trees to get a better view, because when the Spirit moves they fall out!

11. Isobel Rosie Govan, *Spirit of Revival: A Biography of J. G. Govan* (Edinburgh: Faith Mission, 1960), 26.

12. Govan, *Spirit of Revival*, 27.

Chapter 3

1. See Genesis 2:19.
2. Genesis 1:26–28 NKJV.
3. 1 Corinthians 13:7.
4. See Genesis 6:6.
5. See Romans 3:23.
6. See Psalm 8:4–6.
7. Psalm 8:6 NKJV.
8. See Matthew 16:18–19.
9. 1 Peter 2:9.
10. N. T. Wright, *Virtue Reborn* (New York: HarperOne, 2010), 67.
11. Romans 8:28.
12. Luke 22:29.
13. John 12:26.
14. See John 13:5–7.
15. Ephesians 2:6–7.
16. See Exodus 19:9a; Joshua 3:7.
17. See Judges 6:11–12.
18. See 1 Samuel 10:7.
19. Matthew 5:14–16.

Chapter 4

1. Matthew 6:33 THE MESSAGE.

2. The enemy has captured the minds of believers on this issue for a long time. He knows that we overcome him by the blood of the Lamb and the word of our testimony (Revelation 12:11). Since he is afraid of your story, he always seeks to keep you focused on your imperfection instead of your transformation. He knows that what you focus on is what you move toward.

3. I heard this in a talk delivered by Rick Warren but can't recall the date or details.

4. Jeremiah 33:3.

5. The rhythm of the gospel is "come and see," not "come and hear." There ought to be tangible, visible, demonstrable activity of Jesus among us that is immediately discernible to every searching heart. We are not simply inviting people to an event, but to a life-transforming encounter. Events don't change lives—encounters do.

Chapter 5

1. See Luke 15:1–3 THE MESSAGE.

2. See Luke 15:8–10.

3. Quote from a message by Andy Stanley.

4. Acts 15:19.

5. We changed our preferences; we did not change our pursuit of His presence.

6. I love the disciplined focus and intentional bias of those churches and movements that have an irrevocable commitment to reaching their city and who attentively address the needs of their city while providing safe environments for people who are curious about faith but are not yet convinced. I admire their willingness to limit their freedom in worship for the sake of those who are far from God. Mostly I yearn for and honor their effectiveness in embracing the Jesus life of "seeking and saving the lost." We have learned so much from them. Without their example, we would not be seeing dozens of people every month come to Christ. Without them, we would still be drifting inward—doing church for us. These churches and movements have taught us the value of guests to the King.

7. See Matthew 28:18–19.

8. Over time our discomfort grew with a model that seemed at times overly business oriented and consumer focused, while lacking much of the dynamism of the New Testament.

9. I am aware that people use these terms differently. Here is my working definition of *attractional* and *missional*. Anything that happens on church time and territory is attractional. Anything that happens outside church time and territory is missional. Anything that focuses on letting outsiders in is attractional. Anything that catalyses and releases insiders out is missional.

Chapter 6

1. Smith Wigglesworth, *Faith That Prevails* (Radford, VA: Wilder, 2007), 9.

2. Acts 1:8.

3. Acts 2:42–47 NASB.

4. See Acts 8:1.

5. Acts 8:4.

6. Acts 8:5–8.

7. Acts 11:19–21.

8. Acts 11:22.

9. Acts 11:23–24.

10. Acts 13:2–4.

11. See Exodus 3:7–10.

12. See John 3:16.

13. John 20:21b.

14. See John 10:10.

15. See Genesis 2.

16. Dee Hock, *Birth of the Chaordic Age* (San Francisco: Berrett-Koehler, 1999), 9.

Chapter 7

1. Romans 12:1 THE MESSAGE.

2. Romans 12:1.

3. I first heard this phrase in a talk given at our church by my friend and former lecturer Neil Hudson. His book *Imagine Church: Releasing Whole-Life Disciples* develops the theme further.

4. Genesis 2:7–8, 15.

5. See Genesis 2:7–8.

6. Exodus 31:1–5.

7. In most churches, it seems the gifts of God are connected with individuals rather than industries. Yet the Spirit of God forms industries. He breathes life into industries, which in turn breathe life into cities.

8. Psalm 24:1.

9. See Habakkuk 2:14.

Chapter 8

1. See Romans 1:16.

2. Our ineffectiveness at bringing hope to our cities ought to sufficiently humble us to recognize our mistake in divorcing missional and supernatural.

3. We have discovered dreams to be one of the ways God uses to speak into the lives of those who don't yet know Him. So we create environments to help people become more effective in interpreting dreams for unbelievers.

4. See John Wimber's excellent book *Witnesses for a Powerful Christ*.

5. Acts 1:8.

6. I say "Healing on the Streets," but it didn't look anything like Healing on the Streets today. The chairs were uneven, and we had no banner. We made a sign saying "Miracles and Healing at 3:00 p.m." and waited for people to come.

7. 1 Samuel 23:3.

8. Acts 19:10–12, 18–20.

9. Lest we think this is simply the stuff of legend, let's remember John Calvin understood that miracles, signs, and wonders were always particularly present in reaching communities that had previously proven resistant to the gospel.

10. See Luke 13:18–19.

11. Luke 13:10–17.

12. And therefore temporary exclusion from the community.

13. Of course this is exactly what Jesus is driving at … the kingdom is associated with uncleanness just as Jesus Himself associates with the unclean, the outcast.

14. "Ryan Triumphs over Tragedy," *Coleraine Chronicle*, November 10, 2016.

15. "Court Told of Man's Big Lifestyle Change," *Coleraine Chronicle*, May 2015.

16. "Ryan Triumphs over Tragedy."

Chapter 9

1. Paraphrase of Smith Wigglesworth quote.

2. Acts 2:33.

3. Acts 1:1b.

4. The parables of Jesus often describe this reality.

5. A phrase borrowed from the brilliant Dallas Willard.

6. Luke 16:11.

7. Acts 4:33.

8. My paraphrase of Bill Johnson's words, "We owe the world an encounter with God."

9. See 1 Corinthians 14:1.

10. Matthew 13:12 NASB.

11. Ephesians 1:3.

12. See 2 Timothy 2:7 NIVUK.

13. See John 5:19.

14. I acknowledge that sometimes this shows up in our lives simply as a gift—those moments are glorious. But mostly it is the fruit—the predictable outcome—of a kingdom process.

15. Zechariah 4:10 TLB.

16. See Mark 3:3–6.

17. See Mark 5:30–34.

18. See John 9:6–7.

19. Psalm 23:5a.

20. Deuteronomy 3:1–3, 21.

Chapter 10

1. Ephesians 1:1–3.

2. First, we wanted people to show up and support our vision. Second, we looked for people who would serve. Then we realized, for example, that it wasn't enough that people had the will to serve as the worship leader; they also needed skill to serve as the worship leader.

3. The problem with that model for us was that none of it required individuals to know their identity. It's possible to serve wholeheartedly from a posture of guilt rather than grace, from a place of worthlessness rather than wholeness. Yet the service looks the same. Serving from a root of shame retards spiritual growth and masks the identity issues in our lives. We may serve to please others. We may even serve to please God yet never know He is already pleased with us. And all of it is impossible to detect on the surface.

4. Gradually believers were set free from false loyalty to ministry and now exercised ministry knowing their authority. Like Jesus in John 13:1–4, they knew who they were and knew what they carried, so they gladly stepped down and served.

5. Ephesians 3:10.

6. Matthew 10:1, 5–8.

7. For example, the widow's mite and the mustard-seed faith.

8. Matthew 18:20.

9. See 1 Corinthians 15:25.

10. It is simultaneously the authority of a Son with nothing to prove and of a Servant with everything to give.

11. I am so grateful John Wimber awakened to the spiritual authority on his life and pioneered a church movement that brought life to the nations. Had he

not exercised his spiritual authority (and taught others to do likewise), my life, my church, and my city would be significantly impoverished.

12. Ephesians 1:18–23.

13. Ephesians 2:6.

14. Romans 5:17.

15. Romans 5:17b: "How much more will those who receive God's abundant provision of grace and of the gift of righteousness reign in life through the one man, Jesus Christ!"

16. Ephesians 5:14.

17. Ravenhill tells this story in his book *Why Revival Tarries*.

18. It lies outside the scope of this book to enlarge on each of these, but what I've mentioned are some of the most common ways we increase our authority.

19. Matthew 7:21ff.

20. 1 Peter 5:6.

21. Luke 4:14.

22. Matthew 28:18–20.

23. Matthew 16:19.

24. Jeremiah 1:5ff.

25. See Ephesians 2:20–22.

Chapter 11

1. 1 Samuel 22:2.

2. Isaiah 61:4.

3. Mark 6:34 KJV.

4. Mark 1:41 KJV; Matthew 20:34.

5. Matthew 15:32.

6. Rick Warren, "Defining Your Purposes," chapter 5 in *The Purpose Driven Church: Every Church Is Big in God's Eyes* (Grand Rapids, MI: Zondervan, 1995).

7. Compassion cannot be reduced to philanthropy and should not be confused with philanthropy. It is possible to engage in philanthropy and remain untouched, even unchanged. It is impossible to engage in compassion and not be radically altered by the experience. It is possible to practice philanthropy and become proud. It is impossible to sustain compassion without a humble heart.

8. Indeed, as this book asserts throughout, it is impossible to be a biblical community that is both missional and merciful while (intentionally or inadvertently) neglecting or consciously ignoring the supernatural.

9. I first heard this phrase in a talk given at our church by Mark Stibbe.

10. Matthew 10:1 THE MESSAGE.

11. Exodus 3:1–10.

12. Exodus 4:1–5.

13. I am grateful for every community wakening us to the plight of the poor.

14. Acts 10:38.

Chapter 12

1. Wikipedia article on Colesberg.

2. Mark 1:28.

3. Mark 1:33.

4. Mark 1:37.

5. J. Edwin Orr, *The Fervent Prayer: The Worldwide Impact of the Great Awakening of 1858* (Chicago: Moody, 1974), 46–47. It is estimated that over a hundred thousand converts were added to churches during the 1859 revival. Several times in Ulster the judges had no cases to try. Orr writes, "A Coleraine observer stated in an editorial article, 'No one can deny that a change for the better, which all must believe to be permanent, has taken place in the case of hosts of individuals.' In 1860, the Grand Jury of the Coleraine Quarter Sessions was informed that moral and religious reform had reduced crime to almost negligible proportions, there having been only one unimportant case to try."

6. Mark 1:38.

7. John 4:35.

8. John 4:36.

9. John 4:38.

10. Mark 3:8.

Chapter 13

1. Ephesians 1:22–23.

2. Luke 10:1.

3. See Jonah 4:11.

4. This is a reference to a Bob Goff quote.

5. Matthew 21:5.

6. This is from the introduction of the book *The Externally Focused Quest: Becoming the Best Church FOR the Community.* The full quote reads: "Most churches, blatantly or subtly, have an unspoken objective—'How can we be the "best church in our community?"'—and they staff, budget, and plan accordingly.... Becoming an externally focused church is not about becoming the best church in the community. The externally focused church asks, 'How can we be the best church for our community?'"

7. See John 13.

8. Luke 19:42.

9. Jeremiah 29:7 NKJV.

10. Matthew 10:11, 13 NKJV.

11. A generic term used here to represent male and female, fathers and mothers.

Chapter 14

1. A phrase used by and stolen from my friend Pete Greig.

2. Ephesians 1:17.

3. Acts 2:17–18.

4. Ephesians 2:1–7.

5. Ephesians 2:4–5.

6. My paraphrase of Ezekiel 36:26–28.

7. This is a quote from a talk given by Bill Johnson at one of the conferences I attended.

8. 2 Thessalonians 1:11–12.

9. This seems more aligned with the prayer of Jesus: Your kingdom come, your will be done. I for one would feel a lot safer praying that kind of prayer. It's just not the prayer of Paul for this community.

10. See Luke 1:3.

11. It leads to His life filling us and increasing in us, or what Paul calls us being glorified in Him and He in us.

12. 1 Kings 3:5.

13. 1 Kings 3:6–9.

14. 1 Kings 3:10.

15. 1 Kings 3:11–12.

16. 1 Kings 3:11–12.

17. Ephesians 2:10.

18. See Romans 8:28.

19. "God of This City," track 5 on Bluetree, *Greater Things*, Survivor, 2015.

Chapter 15

1. 2 Corinthians 2:14 ESV.

2. Romans 12:1–2.

3. Ephesians 1:20–23 THE MESSAGE.

4. Thanks to Bill Johnson for these thoughts.

5. See Acts 2:2.

6. One of the saddest aspects of settling for cultural relevance is that our cities are not looking for an echo—they are listening for a sound. Our cities need us to be the church with a distinct sound and voice. As we respond to the divine sound, we release its frequency in the community.

7. Bill Johnson, *The Supernatural Power of a Transformed Mind: Access to a Life of Miracles* (Shippensburg, PA: Destiny Image, 2014).

8. 1 Kings 10:1–10.

9. Ephesians 3:20.

10. Revelation 21:3–5.